The SAGE Guide
to Writing in Policing

The SAGE Guide to Writing in Policing

Report Writing Essentials

Jennifer M. Allen
Nova Southeastern University

Steven Hougland
Florida Sheriffs Association

Los Angeles | London | New Delhi
Singapore | Washington DC | Melbourne

FOR INFORMATION:

SAGE Publications, Inc.
2455 Teller Road
Thousand Oaks, California 91320
E-mail: order@sagepub.com

SAGE Publications Ltd.
1 Oliver's Yard
55 City Road
London, EC1Y 1SP
United Kingdom

SAGE Publications India Pvt. Ltd.
B 1/I 1 Mohan Cooperative Industrial Area
Mathura Road, New Delhi 110 044
India

SAGE Publications Asia-Pacific Pte. Ltd.
18 Cross Street #10-10/11/12
China Square Central
Singapore 048423

Printed in the United States of America

Library of Congress Cataloging-in-Publication Data

Names: Allen, Jennifer M., author. | Hougland, Steven M., author.

Title: The SAGE guide to writing in policing: report writing essentials / Jennifer M. Allen, Nova Southeastern University, Steven Hougland, Florida Sheriffs Association.

Description: First edition. | Thousand Oaks, California: SAGE Publications, Inc., [2020] | Includes bibliographical references.

Identifiers: LCCN 2019035158 | ISBN 9781544364643 (paperback) | ISBN 9781544364636 (epub) | ISBN 9781544364629 (epub) | ISBN 9781544364612 (ebook)

Subjects: LCSH: Police reports—United States. | Police—United States—Authorship. | Police administration—Research—United States.

Classification: LCC HV7936.R53 A46 2020 | DDC 808.06/6363—dc23 LC record available at https://lccn.loc.gov/2019035158

This book is printed on acid-free paper.

Acquisitions Editor: Jessica Miller
Editorial Assistant: Sarah Manheim
Marketing Manager: Jillian Ragusa
Production Editor: Veronica Stapleton Hooper
Copy Editor: Karin Rathert
Typesetter: Hurix Digital
Proofreader: Dennis W. Webb
Cover Designer: Candice Harman

MIX
Paper from responsible sources
FSC
www.fsc.org
FSC® C008955

19 20 21 22 23 10 9 8 7 6 5 4 3 2 1

Brief Contents

Detailed Contents

Preface

As practitioners in policing and probation, we saw many reports that did not provide enough information to make a case for court prosecution or treatment and rehabilitation. As educators, we have seen students in criminal justice struggle with writing, citations, referencing, and understanding the processes and procedures of criminal justice without seeing actual reports that mark the progression of a case through the system or the creation of an academic paper. This supplemental text focuses on teaching students how to write in the academic setting, while introducing them to a number of other writing tools, such as memos, emails, resumes, and letters. The goal is to interweave professional and applied writing, academic writing, and information literacy, with the result being a stronger, more confident report writer and student in criminal justice.

There are several challenges to writing in criminal justice: (1) Criminal justice practitioners fail to write for an audience and (2) the use of generic report templates. First, to write effectively, the writer must consider the audience's understanding of the topic and the audience's needs and use of the information. Most practitioners fail to consider that they have an audience beyond their immediate supervisor. As such, reports typically lack detail, are filled with slang and jargon, and are structured in a manner often confusing to those without a criminal justice background. Next, most practitioners are taught to use templates for crime types and court documents. In other words, every burglary report will follow the same format, with a simple adjustment of the case facts. The same is true for other common crime types. So details may be missed or omitted because they do not "fit" the template.

Instructors also sometimes struggle with two issues that are shared by students: (1) writing for fact and (2) brevity. Students and faculty are taught throughout their academic careers to write to page-length requirements. In criminal justice reports, there is not a page-length requirement, and the writing process requires the writer to say what needs to be said factually and succinctly. Thus, students have to train themselves to identify the facts and to learn how to write only what is tangible in a report. Instructors have to find a way to teach these skills, while introducing critical thinking and information literacy. This can be a challenge for everyone involved.

With these concerns in mind, we have written a concise book that introduces key topics in writing in the criminal justice discipline, particularly in policing, and academic writing. We believe the text is reader friendly and comprehensive, yet concise.

Approach

Universities have historically supported intensive courses in writing and have encouraged writing in the discipline across the various academic fields. However, how this has been accomplished is not always clear and varies tremendously from school to school. Sometimes, writing is taught almost exclusively in English courses, while other times, it includes the efforts of individual criminal justice departments. Regardless of the approach, we believe that criminal justice departments have a responsibility to focus on teaching applied writing to their students because writing is an essential skill in this field. In the process of teaching applied writing, instructors can also prepare students to write well academically by introducing information literacy, critical thinking in writing, and the American Psychological Association (APA) style.

The first chapter of this text focuses on the basics of writing by introducing common grammar errors and the types of writing projects commonly seen in academia and the field of criminal justice. The second chapter introduces information literacy and digital literacy to students. Chapter 3 provides information on the police report face page. Chapter 4 continues to focus on police report writing by including explanations of supplemental reports, investigative reports, and traffic accident reports. Affidavits and warrant information is included in Chapter 5. Memos, letters, social media, resumes, and cover letters are described in Chapter 6, along with examples of each. Chapter 7 focuses on plagiarism and APA formatting along with other types of writing styles that students may use in the college setting. The final chapter, Chapter 8, concentrates on the academic research paper by providing students a format to use and information on how to read a scholarly article.

The chapters are enhanced with other features such as

- Chapter summaries

- Narrative and descriptive examples

- Questions for consideration and critical thinking

- In the News reports supporting the material discussed

- Applied exercises

- Examples from common documents used in policing

Acknowledgments

Even though this is the first edition of the text, we have several individuals to thank for their contributions. We thank the following reviewers of the manuscript for their many helpful suggestions:

Shannyn Botsford, Bryant and Stratton College

Julie Brancale, Western Carolina University

Karen Clark, PhD, University of Arizona

Claudia Cox, Teaching Fellow in Criminology and Criminal Justice, Institute of Criminal Justice Studies, University of Portsmouth

Joel M. Cox, Liberty University

Dr. Jean Dawson, Franklin Pierce University

Jeffery Dennis, Minnesota State University

Bryn Herrschaft-Eckman, PhD, Temple University

Milton C. Hill, PhD, Stephen F. Austin State University

Paul "PK" Klenowski, Clarion University of PA

Stephen J. Koonz, MA, LMSW, Dept. of Sociology; SUNY Oneonta

Renee D. Lamphere, UNC Pembroke

Anita Lavorgna, University of Southampton

Jerry W. Lee, Rasmussen College

John P. Mabry, University of Central Oklahoma

Shana L. Maier, Widener University

Iryna Malendevych, University of Central Florida

Carrie Maloney, East Stroudsburg University

Christina Mancini, PhD, Virginia Commonwealth University, Wilder School of Government and Public Affairs

Butch Newkirk, University of North Georgia

Jessica Noble, Lewis and Clark Community College

Matthew Pate, School of Criminal Justice, University at Albany

Elizabeth B. Perkins, PhD, Morehead State University

Selena M. Respass, Miami Dade College

R.D. Robertson, DEA (Retired)

Tiffany J. Samsel, Rowan University

Jeanne Subjack, Southern Utah University

Dr. Mercedes Valadez, Division of Criminal Justice, California State University, Sacramento

Nick Zingo, California State University Northridge

About the Authors

Jennifer M. Allen is a full professor at Nova Southeastern University in the School of Criminal Justice. She has worked with juveniles in detention, on probation, and with those victimized by abuse and neglect. Dr. Allen has served on advisory boards for Big Brother/Big Sister mentoring programs, Rainbow Children's Home, domestic violence/sexual assault programs, and teen courts. Dr. Allen has published in the areas of restorative justice, juvenile delinquency and justice, youth programming, police crime, and police administration and ethics. She is also the co-author of *Criminal Justice Administration: A Service Quality Approach, Juvenile Justice: A Guide to Theory, Policy, and Practice, and The Sage Guide to Writing in Criminal Justice*.

Steven Hougland is a retired law enforcement officer with 30 years of policing experience, a former associate professor of criminal justice, researcher, and author. Dr. Hougland has published in the areas of police use of force, law enforcement accreditation, and police criminality. He is also the author of *The SAGE Guide to Writing in Criminal Justice*.

The Basics of Writing

There is an adage in criminal justice that "if it's not in writing, it didn't happen." This means that criminal justice documents must provide enough details to explain what actually happened at a scene or during an incident or court hearing. Missing details or information that is written vaguely may result in a case being dismissed. Further, a poorly written report could open the door for a mistrial, a not guilty verdict, or the criminal justice worker may appear to have made up the details or to be unsure of the reported details when testifying on the stand. Therefore, it is important that those working in criminal justice understand the complexities of writing quality reports.

Criminal justice officers are required to write many different types of narrative and descriptive documents. In policing, the basic incident report documents the officer's or inmate's activity; records the actions and testimony of victims, suspects, and witnesses; serves as a legal account of an event; and is used for court testimony. Being the best writer possible is a necessity for professionals in the criminal justice field.

The need to write well has never been more important. Relating facts about an incident and investigation go far beyond the eyes of the supervisor and agency. A report will convict criminals, encourage the support of the community, and become a guide by which the public and the courts will measure their respect for the criminal justice system and its workers.

Additionally, criminal justice reports are public record in many states. As such, they are available for all to review. Attorneys, paralegals, and staff personnel on both sides of a case, as well as judges and journalists, may read criminal justice reports. Imagine writing a report that is read by a Justice of the Supreme Court!

Similarly, criminal justice professors often require students to complete writing assignments such as essays, case analyses, and legal briefs. These assignments help develop thinking skills, as well as research and writing skills required in criminal justice careers.

This chapter introduces students to common writing assignments in the criminal justice and criminology classroom, as well as those required in the criminal justice professions.

Basic Grammar Rules

Studies suggest successful writing skills take much longer to develop. Learning to write an effective, extended text is a vastly complex process that often requires more than two decades of training. A skilled, professional writer progresses beyond writing to tell a story to crafting the narrative with the audience's interpretation of the text in mind (Kellogg, 2008). Paragraphs and sentences form the basis of the text. Writing clear, short sentences is an important element of technical writing.

Any discussion on writing begins with the sentence.

The Sentence

The sentence is comprised of a subject and a predicate, and the unit must make complete sense. In other words, a sentence must be able to stand alone as a complete thought. Sentences can be one word or a complex combination of words. Criminal justice professionals write all documents using complete sentences, usually in the first person with no slang or jargon. Sentences should be brief with no structural, grammatical, or spelling errors. The writer must write clear, complete sentences so that the audience can easily understand the writing.

The Subject

The subject is the word that states who or what does the action or is acted upon by the verb. The subject can be expressed or implied. Rephrase the following sentences as questions to identify the subject. So, for number 1, for example, one could ask, "Who reported the crime?" The answer, of course, is the victim, and in this sentence, "victim" functions as the subject.

Examples:

1. The *victim* reported the crime.
   Who reported the crime? The victim.

2. *I* responded to the scene.

3. *I* arrested the defendant.

4. *Deputy Smith* read the defendant his Miranda rights.

5. The *suspect* entered the vehicle through the driver's door.

If a sentence requires a subject and a predicate, can one word function as a complete sentence? Yes, if that word is a command. In a command, the subject is the implied or understood "you."

Examples:

1. "Stop!"

   The subject is not clearly stated, but it is implied or understood to be "you."

2. "Sit down!"

3. "Halt!"

The Verb

The verb is the word or group of words that describes what action is taking place.

Examples:

1. The Deputy *drove*.
   Drove tells what action the subject (Deputy) did.

2. The Deputy *was dispatched* to the call.
   Was dispatched tells what action is taking place.

3. I *arrested* the defendant.

4. *Stop*!
   Remember the subject in a command is the implied "you."

5. I *did not respond* to the call.

Standing Alone and Making Complete Sense

A complete sentence must have a subject and a verb, and it must make complete sense. The sentence must be a complete idea; it must be able to stand alone as a complete thought.

Examples:

Incorrect 1. The agent.

The subject (agent) lacks a verb and does not make complete sense.

Incorrect 2. The agent purchased.

The subject (agent) and verb (purchased) lacks complete sense.

Correct 3. The agent purchased cocaine. (complete sentence)

Incorrect 4. The agent arrested.

The subject (agent) and verb (arrested) lacks complete sense.

Correct 5. The agent arrested the defendant. (complete sentence)

Incorrect 6. The Deputy who responded to the scene. (incomplete sentence)

Correct 7. The Deputy who responded to the scene arrested the defendant. (complete sentence)

Correct 8. The agent was working. (complete sentence)

Correct 9.   The agent was working in an undercover capacity. (complete sentence)

Correct 10.   The agent was working in an undercover capacity for the purpose of purchasing cocaine. (complete sentence)

Exercise 1.1

Identify the subject and verb in each of the following examples:

I arrested the defendant.
　　I (subject) + arrested (verb).

1. The defendant entered the victim's vehicle.

2. The defendant smashed the driver's door window.

3. He removed a stereo from the dash.

4. The stereo is valued at $300.00.

5. I processed the scene for latent prints.

6. The defendant punched the victim in the face.

7. The suspect removed the victim's bicycle from the garage.

8. I responded to the scene.

9. I arrested the defendant.

10. I transported the defendant to Central Booking for processing.

See answers on p. 20.

Structural Errors

Some of the most common structural errors in criminal justice and academic writing are fragments, run-on sentences, and comma splices. But once identified, they are easily corrected.

Fragments

A fragment is an incomplete sentence.
All of the following are fragments:

1. Entered the vehicle. (no subject)

2. Processed the scene. (no subject)

3. I the scene. (no verb)

4. At the scene. (no subject or verb)

5. I processed. (lacks completeness)

Fragments can be corrected in any one of several ways. After identifying the missing element (subject, verb, or completeness), simply insert the missing element to complete the sentence.

Revised 1.   The defendant entered the vehicle.

Revised 2.   A crime scene technician processed the scene.

Revised 3.   I responded to the scene.

Revised 4.   The defendant was found at the scene.

Revised 5.   I processed the scene.

Run-On Sentences

A run-on sentence is two or more complete sentences improperly joined without punctuation.

Example 1: We arrived at the scene Deputy Smith interviewed the victim.

Sentence 1: We arrived at the scene.

Sentence 2: Deputy Smith interviewed the victim.

Revision Strategy 1. Create two independent sentences.

Revision 1. We arrived at the scene. Deputy Smith interviewed the victim.

Revision Strategy 2. Join the independent clauses with a comma and a coordinating conjunction such as *and, but, for, nor, or, so,* or *yet.*

Revision 2. We arrived at the scene, and Deputy Smith interviewed the victim.

Punctuation Alert! Always place the comma *before* the coordinating conjunction.

Revision Strategy 3. Join the independent clauses with a semicolon if they are closely related ideas.

Revision 3. We arrived at the scene; Deputy Smith interviewed the victim.

Comma Splices

A comma splice is two independent clauses joined improperly with a comma.

Example 1. We arrived at the scene, Deputy Smith interviewed the victim.

Revision Strategy 1. Separate the two sentences by adding a comma followed by a coordinating conjunction.

Revised 1. We arrived at the scene, and Deputy Smith interviewed the victim.

Punctuation

All sentences contain punctuation. Punctuation helps the audience understand the writer's meaning.

Let's eat Grandma.
Let's eat, Grandma.

Save a life—use correct punctuation.

Commas

The most frequently used, and misused, punctuation mark is the comma. Use a comma to join two independent clauses with a coordinating conjunction (*and, but, for, or, nor, yet, so*). The comma is always placed *before* the conjunction.

A comma is used to separate a dependent clause from the independent clause:

Example 1:

1. I arrested the defendant, and I booked him into the jail.

Two independent clauses:

1. I arrested the defendant.
2. I booked him into the jail.

A comma is required before the coordinating conjunction.

2. I arrested the defendant and booked him into the jail.
   1. One independent clause: I arrested the defendant.
   2. One dependent clause: booked him into the jail. (no subject)

A comma is not used.

More Examples:

1. I interviewed the victim, and she gave a sworn statement.
2. I interviewed the victim, but she refused to give a sworn statement.

A comma is used to separate items in a list. Place a comma before the *and* at the end of the series.

Examples:

1. Deputies Smith, Jones, and White responded to the call. (correct)

2. Deputies Smith, Jones and White responded to the call. (incorrect)

Commas are also used after conjunctive adverbs (however, therefore, and so on). However, if the phrase is very short—less than three words—the comma may be omitted.

Examples:

1. When I responded to the call, I activated my emergency lights and siren.

2. Responding to the call, I activated my emergency lights and siren.

3. Therefore, the findings of my investigation are that no crime took place.

A comma is used to isolate an appositive (a phrase that renames the noun).

Examples:

1. The man, a white male, was arrested for theft.

2. Deputy Smith, a rookie, was assigned to the midnight shift.

3. My assigned vehicle, car 1042, is a 1991 Ford LTD.

Check if the commas have been placed properly by simply removing the words between the commas. If what remains is a complete sentence, the commas are correctly placed.

Example:

The man, a white male, was arrested for theft.

Remove the words between the commas: a white male.

What remains, "The man was arrested for theft" is a complete sentence.

The placement of the commas is correct.

Exercise 1.2

Place or remove commas for correct punctuation.

1. We approached the defendant and Deputy Smith asked to buy a "dime."

2. We approached the defendant, and asked to buy a "dime."

3. At today's Day-Shift briefing Sergeant Jones asked for volunteers.

4. I charged the defendant with sale and delivery of cocaine, possession of cocaine and possession of drug paraphernalia.

5. Sergeant Jones the Day-Shift supervisor, asked for volunteers.

6. I arrested the defendant for shoplifting yet he denied the charge.

7. I am usually assigned to Zone 43 but today I am working in Zone 45.

8. Today I wrote reports for burglary, theft and battery.

9. Deputy Smith, an experienced agent made a cocaine seizure today.

See answers on p. 20.

The Semicolon

The semicolon indicates a strong relationship between two sentences. Examples:

1. I interviewed the victim; however, she failed to provide a statement.

2. I arrested the defendant; later, I transported and booked him into the jail.

Exercise 1.3

Insert or remove semicolons for correct punctuation.

1. We responded to the call, Deputy Smith wrote the report.

2. At briefing the sergeant asked for; volunteers and reports.

3. I saw the rescue team treating the victim. She had a stomach wound.

4. The defendant removed the item from the shelf, she then left the store after failing to pay.

5. I am assigned to Sector 4, and I primarily work Zone 43.

See answers on p. 21.

The Colon

The colon is used to introduce a list.

Examples:

1. The defendant was charged with the following: burglary, grand theft, and criminal mischief.
   (Notice the placement of the commas in the series.)

2. Three Deputies responded to the call: Smith, Jones, and Harris.

Exercise 1.4

Insert colons appropriately.

1. I charged the defendant with the following, assault, battery, and theft.

2. The following attachments are provided with this report, sworn statements, tow sheet, and evidence form.

3. I testified on several cases today while in court 92-123456, 90-123456, and 89-123456.

See answers on p. 21.

Quotation Marks

Quotation marks are used to indicate another person's spoken or written words. They are useful in criminal justice documents to indicate statements made by suspects or defendants, responses or comments by victims or witnesses that are particularly relevant to an investigation, or anytime an important statement is made. Students also regularly use quotation marks in their academic papers. However, it is important to remember to only quote from a source when the information cannot be paraphrased in another way, it involves statistics that must be stated exactly, or the point is so important that a student believes it must be stated exactly as the original author wrote. Students should always use quoted material sparingly and attempt to paraphrase or summarize the work as much as possible.

If the quotation is placed at the end of the sentence, a comma is placed before the opening quotation mark. A period is placed within the end quotation mark at the end of the sentence after the in-text citation:

Examples:

1. The defendant stated, "I didn't mean to kill her."

2. I told the defendant, "You're under arrest."

If a sentence begins with a quotation, a comma is placed within the end quotation mark.

3. "I didn't mean to kill her," he said.

If a quotation mark is around a single word or group of words, the punctuation *always* goes inside the quotation mark:

Examples:

1. I asked the suspect if he knew where I could purchase a "dime," the common street reference for $10 of cocaine.

2. The victim told me he had taken LSD and was "high," so I called Rescue for medical treatment.

Exercise 1.5

Punctuate the following sentences properly using quotation marks and commas as needed.

1. The victim said He stabbed me in the stomach.

2. He stabbed me in the stomach she said.

3. I bought three hits of LSD today.

4. Today I bought three hits of LSD two cocaine rocks and a gram of pot.

5. I asked the defendant for a dime and he took me to 1234 18th Street in Zone 42.

6. She said He stabbed me in the stomach; but I saw no wound.

7. The deputy asked, Who called the Police?

8. Who was it who said Live and let live?

See answers on p. 21.

Plurals

Many nouns are changed to the plural form simply by adding an s or *es* to the end of the noun: *Officer* becomes *officers*; *bus* becomes *buses*. Some nouns, however, form plurals irregularly by changing the spelling of the word. Some of the most common include the following:

man men   woman women   me us I we

Some nouns do not change their spelling at all to form plurals: *deer, sheep, fish, police.*

Some nouns that have a Latin root still use the Latin form of the plural rather than the English *s*. Some examples include *datum/data*, *crisis/crises*, and *memorandum/memoranda*.

Possessives

The possessive form demonstrates a relationship between two nouns.

Examples:

1. The victim's car was burglarized.

2. The defendant's rights were revoked.

3. The vehicle's tires were slashed.

If the noun is plural and ends with an *s*, add only an apostrophe.

Examples:

1. The victims' cars were burglarized.

2. The defendants' rights were revoked.

3. These are the victims' radios.

4. Here are the officers' guns.

5. The vehicles' tires were slashed.

Capitalization

Capitalize the names of directions when they indicate a specific location, but not when they indicate a general direction.

Examples:

1. South Carolina

2. The defendant fled south on foot.

Capitalize titles only when they precede the person's name.

Examples:

1. Colonel Smith

2. I met with the colonel.

Commonly Misused Words

Homophones are words that look and sound alike but have different meanings. The following are examples of homophones:

Its and *it's*

1. *Its* shows possession. "You can't judge a book by its cover."

2. *It's* is the contraction of *it is*.

There, *their*, and *they're*

1. *There* indicates a location. An easy way to remember this is to look for the word *here* within *there*. *There* also functions as an adverb, as in "There are no more calls holding."

2. *Their* is an adjective. It describes a noun by showing that an object belongs to more than one person or thing: "Their car was burglarized," or "Here is their stolen property," or "The dogs were in their pen."

3. *They're* is the contraction of *they are*.

Lie, *lay*, *lain*: to recline

1. I will now lie down.

2. Yesterday I lay down.

3. Last week, I had also lain down.

Lay, *laid*, *laid*; to place or set down

1. I will now lay my book down.

2. He laid the gun on the ground.

3. He had already laid his gun down.

Who and *whom*

Who is used as the subject; *whom* is used as an object.

1. Who wrote the report?

2. The Lieutenant asked the Sergeant, "Whom did you have write this report?"

In modern, spoken English, *whom* is rarely used.
Which, *who*, and *that*

1. The horses, which were kept at the stable, jumped the fence to get loose.

2. The Deputies who responded to the call took 2 minutes to arrive.

The Modifier

A modifier is a word or group of words that describes a noun or a verb. Modifiers may appear before or after the word they describe, but the modifier must be logically placed to prevent confusion.

Exercise 1.6

Insert the correct word.

1. A police patrol car is easily identified by (it's/its) _____ distinctive color scheme.

2. When is shift change? (It's/Its) _____ this weekend.

3. Yes, (there/their/they're) _____ are no bananas.

4. We are going over (there/their/they're) _____.

5. We found (there/their/they're) _____ stolen property.

6. (There/Their/They're) _____ going over (there/their/they're) _____.

7. I will (lie/lay/lain) _____ down now.

8. The suspect (lay/laid) _____ the gun on the ground, and the officer ordered him to (lie, lay, lain) _____ face down.

9. (Who/Whom) _____ responded to the call?

10. Deputy Smith, (who/whom) _____ did you interview at the scene?

11. The people (which/who/that) _____ were arrested during the reverse sting operation were all adults.

See answers on p. 21.

Examples:

1. Officer Smith's decision to transfer was an *important* career move.

2. The crime scene perimeter was planned *carefully* by the sergeant.

Notice that the modifiers in both sentences can be dropped without changing the meaning of the sentence.

1. Officer Smith's decision to transfer was a career move.

2. The crime scene perimeter was planned by the sergeant.

Modifiers can easily confuse readers when they are misplaced within a sentence.

Examples:

1. Suffering from a heart attack, Deputy Smith found the victim at her door. (Who had the heart attack?)

Revised

1. Deputy Smith found the victim at her door suffering from a heart attack.

Examples:

Misplaced 1: The female Deputy, while searching the female informant, found the drugs that were sold by Deputy Smith in the woman's pants.

Revised 1: The female Deputy, while searching the female informant, found the drugs in the woman's pants. The drugs were sold by Deputy Smith in the reverse sting operation.

Misplaced 2: Deputy Jones, while on routine patrol, saw the drunk driver who was arrested by Deputy Harris driving south on Kirkman Road.

Revised 2: Deputy Jones, while on routine patrol, saw the drunk driver driving south on Kirkman Road. Deputy Harris arrested the drunk driver.

Spelling

Proper spelling is a vital part of every written document. Just as improper grammar and punctuation is a sign of semi-literacy, so too is improper spelling. A misspelled word screams for the reader's attention and shapes a negative image of the writer. Several misspelled words can have such a negative effect upon the reader that many will simply refuse to continue reading, finding it too difficult to understand the narrative.

Those who write by hand should keep a good dictionary nearby. When writing by computer, do not overly rely on the spell check. While a spell check will identify and correct misspelled words, it will fail to correct homophones. In this sentence, *four* example, the word "for" is misspelled as "four," yet a spell check program would fail to identify the error.

The following is a list of the some of the most frequently misspelled words used in criminal justice writing.

accept	attack	disturbance	misdemeanor
accurate	attorney	efficient	paraphernalia
accuse	battery	examination	receive
acquaintance	bruise	fellatio	sergeant
advisable	bureau	felony	sheriff
aggravated	burglary	foreign	subpoena
apparent	canvassed	harass	tattoo
appeal	cemetery	height	trafficking
apprehend	commit	homicide	trespass
apprehension	conceal	interrogate	trying
approximate	confidential	intoxication	unnecessary
argument	conveyance	jewelry	vicinity
armed robbery	counsel	judge	victim
arraignment	criminal	juvenile	warrant
assault	cunnilingus	lieutenant	weight
associate	discipline	marijuana	wounded

Critical Thinking Skills, Academic Writing, and Professional Writing

Being able to identify errors in writing and to write thorough reports and interesting academic papers requires the ability to critically think. A critical thinker will write better because he or she will weed out nonessential information from written documents. Rugerrio (2008) defines critical thinking as "the process by which we test claims and arguments and determine which have merit and which do not" (p. 18). Ennis (2011) adds, "Critical thinking is reasonable, reflective thinking that is focused on deciding what to believe or do" (p. 1). Critical thinking is a foundational goal of the college experience because it is at the core of modern personal, social, and professional life (Paul, 1995). Phillips and Burrell (2009) note critical thinkers overcome biases and false assumptions that impede decision-making. As such, critical thinking prepares students for all aspects of life.

Academic writing enhances critical thinking in several key ways. It is a process that requires students to verify the credibility and biases of source material and objectively examine not just their thoughts and beliefs but also the ideas of those diametrically opposed to their own (Paul, 1995).

Critical thinking is also an essential skill in the criminal justice professions since it is a key piece of problem solving. Common writing assignments in criminal justice classes include a reflective journal, essay paper, research essay, monograph, annotated bibliography, case study, and legal analysis.

Reflective Journal

The reflective journal assignment is designed to capture a student's feelings and responses to an issue. Journals are more than a synopsis or a simple "I think" response to a question. This assignment requires students to thoroughly and critically evaluate a reading assignment by applying current theory, practice, and course materials to assess a problem, issue, or policy.

Essay Paper

A common assignment for students is the essay paper. The narrative and descriptive essay are examples that require no outside research. For these essays, students are asked to tell a story, explain a process, or describe a place or thing. The length of this essay is typically five pages or less, but length can vary according to the course and instructor.

Research Paper

Like the essay paper, the research paper is a commonly assigned project, especially in upper-level courses. Here, students must conduct outside research to identify source materials that either support or refute a thesis. The student must critically analyze sources to ensure the information is from a respected and reliable source and is both current and credible. Although many students feel anxious about writing a research paper, it can be a valuable experience since "many students will continue to do research throughout their career" (Purdue Owl, 2018a).

Monograph

A monograph is an in-depth study of a single subject written by faculty or scholars for an academic audience (Eastern Illinois University, 2016). According to Crossick (2016), the monograph allows for the "full examination of a topic . . . woven together in a reflective narrative that is not possible in a journal article" (p. 15).

Annotated Bibliography

While a bibliography is a list of sources used to research a particular topic or phenomenon, an annotated bibliography provides a summary and evaluation of each source (Purdue OWL, 2018e). The annotated bibliography will include a formatted reference, such as those found in a bibliography, followed by an annotation. Annotations are written in paragraph form and include a summary of the main points of the article; an assessment of how the article relates to the topic, phenomenon, or research question, and a reflection of what may be missing from the article and/or if the source is reliable, biased, and what the goal of the article may be (Purdue OWL, 2018a).

Case Study

A case study is an in-depth analysis of real life events intended to examine individuals, groups, or events in their natural environment (Hancock & Algozzine, 2016). To successfully complete the assignment in criminal justice courses, students are often required to (1) summarize an actual event and identify a problem; (2) provide a detailed explanation of how the problem was addressed or resolved; and (3) critically analyze the resolution by applying course materials, criminal justice theory, and the findings and conclusions of research from previous study of the same or a similar problem.

Legal Analysis

The legal analysis assignment is a research paper in which a student must analyze a set of facts within the context of applicable law. Professors often assign a case study as part of a Constitutional law, state law, or civil law course. Students are required to research judicial opinions, state statutes and constitutions, the United States Constitution, and administrative law (Rowe, 2009). It is particularly important for students to ensure the applied law is not outdated or appealed (Rowe, 2009).

Writing for the Criminal Justice Professions

Thinking critically and writing for academic classes is great practice for the profession of criminal justice. Similarly, the criminal justice professions require a variety of written work. Harvey (2015) notes the most powerful instrument a criminal justice officer carries is a pen. These are strong words considering the many weapons carried by criminal justice practitioners. If a report is poorly written, readers are less likely to take the content seriously and may question the writer's credibility, which, in the criminal justice system, can have serious consequences (Harrison, Weisman, & Zornado, 2017). The following is a short listing of the legal consequences of poorly written reports:

1. Drug case dismissed and inmates released due to bad search warrant (Astolfi, 2016).

2. Killers go free due to incomplete police reports (Haner, Wilson, & O'Donnell, 2002).

3. Police Credibility on Trial in D.C. Courts Drawing the jury's attention to such a discrepancy—by having an officer read aloud from his arrest report—gives a defense lawyer an opening to explore whether the officer might have been wrong about other important facts (Flaherty & Harriston, 1994).

4. Words Used in Sexual Assault Reports Can Hurt Cases

   Poorly written reports—sometimes laden with implications of disbelief or skepticism—can contaminate a jury's perception of a victim's credibility or cripple a case altogether (Dissell, 2010).

5. Officers Indicted by Federal Grand Jury

   Three GA officers charged with writing false reports to cover up police assault (Department of Justice, 2014).

Policing Reports

Police officers are required to write a narrative in many different types of documents. Many agencies use a cover page of check boxes and blank spaces to indicate the type of incident being documented, demographic information, and the address of the parties involved. Many of these same documents, though, require the officer to complete a detailed, written narrative that accurately documents the officer's observations and actions; statements made by victims, witnesses, and suspects; any evidence collected; and other information relevant to the case. Policing documents are often written in a narrative format in which the officer tells a story of his or her involvement in an official event.

The following writing assignments represent the most often used documents that require a written narrative.

Field Notes

Field notes are commonly used in policing. Notes taken at a crime scene are vital to the accuracy of initial and follow-up reports. Officers are also able to refer to their field notes to refresh their memory during deposition and trial in most states. Note taking is the process of gathering and recording facts and information relevant to the police investigation. Officers gather a variety of information in a quick and efficient manner, so they may recall the facts of the case to write the incident report, assist follow-up investigations, and refresh their memory for court testimony.

Incident Reports

The incident report is the most common type of writing assignment in policing. It is usually written by a patrol officer to officially document a crime reported by a citizen or when the officer makes an arrest. The document serves several purposes. It is a legal document of an officer's actions, observations, and conversations at a crime scene or self-initiated contact with a citizen. Typical reports can range from one to three pages in length, but more serious crimes are often five or more pages. Incident reports are used by investigators, prosecutors, defense attorneys, judges, and the media to evaluate an officer's job performance.

Supplemental Report

This report is an addendum to the incident report. The supplemental report is often used by officers and investigators to add additional information to the incident report. The supplemental report is most often used to document interviews, evidence collected, or other activity related to a case that occurred after an officer's original incident report.

Booking Reports

In addition to an incident report, officers are often required to write a booking report when an arrestee is transported or delivered to a jail. The narrative of a booking report is often just two or three paragraphs since it requires only the details that establish probable cause for the arrest.

Evidence

The evidence report is used to document any item that has been seized by an officer or has evidentiary value. It also establishes a chain of custody so that seized items can be presented in court. Advances in the technology available to criminal justice agencies have expanded the scope of items of evidentiary value to include video and audio recorded on cell phones, body and in-car cameras, housing unit cameras located in adult and juvenile detention facilities, courtroom cameras, and surveillance cameras. This report is also an addendum to the incident report.

Search Warrant

The Fourth Amendment protects against unreasonable searches and seizures, and in general, a search warrant is needed prior to conducting a search. A search warrant is a written order, signed by a judge and issued upon probable cause, to bring the seized property before the court.

The search warrant is a written order, signed by a magistrate having jurisdiction over the place to be searched, based upon probable cause, ordering a police officer to search a particular person or place, and to seize certain described property. The search warrant must sufficiently describe the place to be searched and the items to be seized very clearly so that any officer executing the warrant would make no mistake locating the property or seizing the proper items.

Grants

Many local criminal justice agencies struggle to continue to offer a level of service enjoyed in the past as revenues shrink and budgets are dramatically reduced. There will always be crime, but criminal justice professionals and professors alike are often forced to find new funding sources to create or test new ideas and programs (Davis, 1999).

Perhaps not often enough, these agencies seek out grant funding to supplement personnel and equipment costs, finance community service programs, and fund new initiatives that otherwise would not be possible. According to Karsh and Fox (2014), a grant "is an award of money that allows you to do very specific things that usually meet very specific guidelines that are spelled out in painstaking detail and to which you must respond very clearly in your grant proposal" (p. 12). The field of criminal justice—academically and professionally—has benefited greatly from grant funding (Davis, 1999).

Grant funds can come from a number of sources, including the federal government, corporations, foundations, and even individuals. The federal government, through Grants.gov, is the most prominent grant provider for criminal justice agencies. The United States Department of Justice (DOJ) offers grant funding to local and state law enforcement agencies to "assist victims of crime; to provide training and technical assistance; to conduct research; and to implement programs that improve the criminal, civil, and juvenile justice systems" (DOJ, 2018). Through the Office of Community Oriented Policing, the Office of Justice Systems, and the Office of Violence Against Women, the DOJ provides grants to support the hiring and training of police officers, implementation of crime control programs, and reduction of violence against women (DOJ, 2018). Similarly, the Bureau of Justice Assistance provides grant funding for "law enforcement, prosecution, indigent defense, courts, crime prevention and education, corrections and community corrections, [and] drug treatment" (Office of Justice Programs, 2018). Criminal justice agencies can also establish partnerships with academic institutions.

CHAPTER SUMMARY

Writing well is an important skill for criminal justice students and professionals. Academic writing assignments improve the student's research, critical thinking, and writing skills in preparation for future criminal justice careers. Poor writing can discredit a student, officer, and/or a criminal justice agency's reputation.

Common writing assignments for criminal justice students include essays, case studies, annotated bibliographies, and legal analysis. In addition to gaining a deeper understanding of criminal justice topics and current issues, assignments such as these enhance critical thinking skills, an essential skill in the criminal justice professions since it is a key piece of problem solving.

Criminal justice professionals are required to write a variety of report narratives, such as an incident report, search warrant, grant, or pre-trial report. As Harrison, Weisman, and Zornado (2017) aptly note, a poorly written report may bring into question the writer's credibility, which, in the criminal justice system, can have serious consequences.

ADDITIONAL READING

Strunk, W. (2011). *The elements of style*. Project Gutenberg. Retrieved from https://www.gutenberg.org/files/37134/37134-h/37134-h.htm.

Purdue Online Writing Lab. (2018). General writing resources. Retrieved from https://owl.english.purdue.edu/owl/section/1/.

QUESTIONS FOR CONSIDERATION

1. Why is writing well important in criminal justice professions?

2. What functions do the basic incident report serve?

3. Who might read an incident report inside the criminal justice agency? Outside the agency?

4. Define critical thinking. How is critical thinking important to criminal justice students and practitioners?

5. List three documents commonly used in criminal justice agencies. Describe how these documents are used and why they are important.

EXERCISE ANSWERS

Exercise 1.1 Answers

1. defendant (subject), entered (verb).

2. defendant (subject), smashed (verb).

3. He (subject), removed (verb).

4. stereo (subject), is valued (verb).

5. I (subject), processed (verb).

6. defendant (subject), punched (verb).

7. suspect (subject), removed (verb).

8. I (subject), responded (verb).

9. I (subject), arrested (verb).

10. I (subject), transported (verb).

Exercise 1.2 Answers

1. We approached the defendant, and Deputy Smith asked to buy a "dime."

2. We approached the defendant and asked to buy a "dime."

3. At today's Day-Shift briefing, Sergeant Jones asked for volunteers.

4. I charged the defendant with sale and delivery of cocaine, possession of cocaine, and possession of drug paraphernalia.

5. Sergeant Jones, the Day-Shift supervisor, asked for volunteers.

6. I arrested the defendant for shoplifting, yet he denied the charge.

7. I am usually assigned to Zone 43, but today I am working in Zone 45.

8. Today I wrote reports for burglary, theft, and battery.

9. Deputy Smith, an experienced drug agent, made a cocaine seizure today.

Exercise 1.3 Answers

1. We responded to the call; Deputy Smith wrote the report.

2. At briefing the sergeant asked for volunteers and reports.

3. I saw Rescue treating the victim; she had a stomach wound.

4. The defendant removed the item from the shelf; she then left the store after failing to pay.

5. I am assigned to Sector 4; I primarily work Zone 43.

Exercise 1.4 Answers

1. I charged the defendant with the following: assault, battery, and theft.

2. The following attachments are provided with this report: sworn statements, tow sheet, and evidence form.

3. I testified on several cases today while in court: 92-123456, 90-123456, and 89-123456.

Exercise 1.5 Answers

1. The victim said, "He stabbed me in the stomach."

2. "He stabbed me in the stomach," she said.

3. "I bought three hits of LSD today."

4. "Today I bought three hits of LSD, two cocaine rocks, and a gram of pot."

5. "I asked the defendant for a dime, and he took me to 1234 18th Street in Zone 42."

6. She said, "He stabbed me in the stomach"; but I saw no wound.

7. The deputy asked, "Who called the police?"

8. Who was it who said "Live and let live"?

Exercise 1.6 Answers

1. its

2. it's

3. there

4. there

5. their

6. they're, there

7. lie

8. laid, lie

9. who

10. whom

11. who

CHAPTER 2

What Is Information Literacy?

The average person is bombarded with the equivalent of 174 newspapers of data each day (Alleyne, 2011). The Internet, television, and mobile phones have increased the amount of information a person receives by 5 times as compared to 1986 (Alleyne, 2011). According to researchers at the University of Southern California, the digital age allows people to send out more information by email, twitter, social networking sites, and text messages than at any other time in history. In 1986, each individual generated approximately two and half pages of information a day; however, in 2007, each person produced the equivalent of six, 85-page newspapers daily (Hilbert & Lopez, 2011). Imagine how that may have changed in the last decade! As one can guess, all of this information has to be stored and catalogued. It also has to be analyzed and sorted using our own interpretations and those presented by the media and other outlets. In a world where fake news and social media dominate most of what people read and hear each day, individuals have to be more savvy and use more critical thinking than ever in determining good information from bad information. Individuals also have to be skilled in acquiring facts and in deciding when information is needed and what to take from the data they gather. In other words, people have to be competent in *information literacy*. In this chapter, information literacy will be defined, and the skills needed to become an information literate person will be identified. Additionally, information literacy and its relationship to technology and critical thinking will be discussed. Examples of how information literacy is used in criminal justice will be provided throughout the chapter.

Information Literacy

Information literacy is not just another buzzword. It is a skill that people can develop over time with the proper understanding of research, analysis, and writing. Information literacy is a crucial talent in the pursuit of knowledge, and it is required in the professional world. It is important in workforces that require lifelong learning, like criminal justice, and it is seen as a linking pin to economic development in education, business, and government (The National Forum on Information Literacy, 2018). The National Forum for Information Literacy, sponsored by the American Library Association (2018, para. 3), defined information literacy as a person's ability to "know when they need information, to identify information that can help them address the issue or problem at hand, and to locate, evaluate, and use that information effectively." Most colleges and universities recognize that students should be informationally literate when they graduate. In fact, in 2000, the Association of Colleges and Research Libraries developed the Information Literacy Competency Standards for Higher Education, and in 2004, the American Association for Higher Education and the Council of Independent Colleges endorsed the standards (Stanford's Key to Information Literacy, 2018). Information literacy is considered a key objective for many university and discipline-specific accrediting bodies. Supporting this goal is the belief that information literacy is linked to critical thinking (another objective commanded by colleges and accrediting agencies) because the two skills appear to share very common objectives (Breivik, 2005).

Like information literacy, critical thinking skills require individuals to explore and evaluate ideas for the purpose of forming opinions, problem-solving, and making decisions (Wertz et al., 2013). It has been argued that in both critical thinking and information literacy, individuals must collect information and evaluate its quality and relevance. Then, the individuals must integrate the information into their current understandings or belief systems on particular topics. Finally, in both critical thinking and information literacy, individuals must use the information to draw conclusions and understand the limitations of the information on those conclusions (Wertz et al., 2013). According to Wertz et al. (2013), doing all of this allows for effective decision making.

Other researchers, like Breivik (2005), have argued that it requires critical thinking skills to be information literate because individuals need to analytically assess the information overload they encounter when using technology. Further, a study of digital classrooms in Hong Kong (Kong, 2014) found that using digital classrooms to enhance domain knowledge also increased critical thinking skills among secondary students in a 13-week trial period. However, not all researchers are convinced there is a direct correlation between information literacy and critical thinking. Ward (2006) argued that information literacy goes beyond critical thinking by forcing individuals to manage information in creative and meaningful ways, not to just analyze it. Albitz (2007) claimed that information literacy is skill based, while critical thinking requires higher-order cognitive processes. Finally, Weiler (2005) stated that students in the early years of college may be able to find and access information but may not yet have the ability to critically analyze it because they have not developed beyond a dualistic intellectual capacity. Thus, even though a student may find the information needed, he or she may wait for an authority figure, like a professor, to tell them the answer to the problem. The actual relationship between information literacy and critical thinking skills may well be a chicken and an egg argument wherein the question is if a person needs critical thinking skills to develop information literacy or if information literacy can increase critical thinking skills. It is likely that the two are intertwined. Regardless of the answer to this question, there appears to be enough evidence to convince universities and accrediting bodies that both skills are absolutely required to produce effective, productive, and successful students and employees.

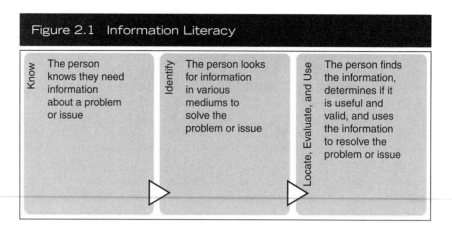

Figure 2.1   Information Literacy

Know	Identify	Locate, Evaluate, and Use
The person knows they need information about a problem or issue	The person looks for information in various mediums to solve the problem or issue	The person finds the information, determines if it is useful and valid, and uses the information to resolve the problem or issue

Just like students are expected to use critical thinking in their academic work, information literacy is common today in all academic disciplines and is used in all learning environments. Many times, students are exposed to activities in classrooms that are designed to build skills in information literacy without even realizing it. Most students in college have probably used information literacy to write a research paper or to respond to a class assignment. But gathering information on a single topic does not just stop there. The information has to be analyzed for usefulness and presented in a way that solves a problem or provides more focus to an issue. Information literacy requires that one also uses the information gathered in ethical and legal ways and that he or she assumes greater control over the investigation and becomes more self-directed in the pursuit of knowledge (The Association of College and Research Libraries, 2000). In fact, the Information Literacy Competency Standards for Higher Education require that an information literate person

1. Determine the extent of information needed

2. Access the needed information effectively and efficiently

3. Evaluate information and its sources critically

4. Incorporate selected information into one's knowledge base

5. Use information effectively to accomplish a specific purpose

6. Understand the economic, legal, and social issues surrounding the use of information, and access and use information ethically and legally (The Association of College and Research Libraries, 2000, pp. 2–3)

Information literacy is related to information technology skills and extends beyond reading a book or listening to the news. Information literacy includes the technology-enriched digital information world. People use *digital literacy skills* when they rely on technology to communicate with family and friends; *computer literacy skills* when they use hardware, software, peripherals, and network components; and *technology literacy* to work independently and with others to effectively use electronic tools to access, manage, integrate, evaluate, create, and communicate information (Stanford's Key to Information Literacy, 2018). Each of these skills is interwoven with and overlap the broader concept of information literacy, as informationally literate individuals will inevitably develop skills in technology during their pursuit of information.

Using Information Literacy—Know, Identify, Evaluate, and Use

As suggested by the Information Literacy Competency Standards for Higher Education (The Association of College and Research Libraries, 2000), information literate individuals will follow a process in identifying and using information to resolve problems or issues. This process requires the person to know, identify, evaluate, and use information effectively, ethically, and legally. This process is summarized in the paragraphs that follow.

Know of a Problem or Issue That Needs to Be Resolved

A person may become aware of a problem or issue in a variety of ways. The person may experience a situation that bothers him or her and makes the individual want to resolve it so no one else experiences the same situation. Consider the case of Megan Kanka, who was kidnapped, sexually assaulted, and murdered by a man who had two previous convictions for sexual offenses. He moved into a home directly across the street from Megan prior to the crime. Neither Megan's parents nor their neighbors knew of his background. After her murder and the efforts of her parents to prevent similar crimes in other areas, Megan's Law was passed. Megan's Law created a sex offender notification system, which provides information on sex offenders to communities when a potentially dangerous sex offender moves into the neighborhood (Larson, 2016). Every state now tracks sex offenders and provides information to the public on them.

A person may be told that there is a problem or issue—perhaps through a meeting (i.e., the police chief is told by the city council that the city is freezing the budget so he cannot hire new police officers), by constituents (i.e., a citizen writes a letter to the mayor complaining that local neighborhood kids are hanging out at the corner stop sign past midnight), on the news or through social media (i.e., a friend posts a video of a person abusing an animal on Facebook), or by noticing a pattern in data (i.e., crime statistics show increases in public intoxication rates during spring break each year). A student, for example, may be told to complete an assignment by a teacher that seeks to solve a problem or make recommendations about a social issue, like child abuse. Knowing about the problem or issue allows for the process of information literacy to start.

Identify Information

Once a person is aware that there is a problem or issue that he or she needs to resolve, the individual will begin the information gathering process. There are a couple of avenues a person may choose to gather information.

He or she may use an information retrieval system, like the library or a database. A police officer, for example, may identify a high-risk area for homelessness by using the spatial statistics program, CrimStat, which analyzes crime by location. Another option is for a person to use lab-based activities or simulations to gather information. For example, to identify weaknesses in emergency preparedness, a policing agency may hold mock emergency scenarios that replicate terrorist attacks on a seaport or a building. A third approach may be for the person to use an investigative technique, like surveys or interviews. For example, a community policing officer may go from business to business in his assigned neighborhood talking with business owners about concerns or issues they are having with local citizens. Once the officer learns that young people are troublesome to business owners because they are hanging around the outside of businesses and harassing potential business customers, he can decide what to do with the remarks. Physical examination can also be used to gather information. Viewing and photographing a crime scene firsthand or witnessing an event with your own eyes can provide a wealth of information about an issue or problem. As an example, a complainant may call the police department to report behaviors similar to prostitution in a local neighborhood. Rather than taking the citizen's word, a police chief may have police officers stake out the neighborhood in undercover cars and/or solicit a potential prostitute, so they can witness the illegal behaviors for themselves. Witnessing the solicitation provides the information needed for the police to evaluate and determine the best course of action for the criminal activity.

Evaluate the Information

The person who is adept at information literacy will find the information he or she is looking for using various mediums, as discussed above. Then, the person will evaluate the abundant pieces of information found. In the evaluation process, the person is tasked with trying to determine whether the information is valid and reliable. The sources of the information should be examined critically to determine if the source is credible. To do this, the Center for Disease Control and Prevention (n.d.) suggests that the information literate person assess the information by asking several questions:

1. **Where did the information come from?** This consideration is focused exclusively on the source of the information. In the case of information retrieval systems, the person may assess the journal article and the journal in which the article was published. The information literate person may read the introduction of the journal to determine if the journal is scientific and if the article was peer reviewed. Knowing that an article that undergoes peer review is much more reliable than an article published in a magazine allows the information literate person to accept the information in the article as trustworthy. Using an example from above, the police officer who evaluates crime data provided by CrimStat and who is familiar with the validity and reliability of these data can make a logical and well-informed decision about how best to handle the increasing number of homeless person arrests.

2. **How does the new information fit with what is already known about the problem or issue?** The police officer who visited businesses to gather information about issues or problems may want to compare juvenile arrest rates for loitering and trespassing from CrimStat to what the business owners are saying. He may also want to talk to other police officers who work in the area to see if they are telling youth to "move along" from businesses throughout the day. Comparing the various pieces of information to one another and to information that was gathered previously allows the individual to determine which pieces of data to keep and which to discard. If the officer has worked as a community policing officer in the area for a while, he may already know where the young people in the community gather.

3. **Is funding involved in the creation of the information?** Although funding may not be a part of every equation in solving an issue or problem, the ability to report findings in a study without bias can be skewed if the researcher writing the report has been funded by an outside source. In other words, the source of the funding for a research project may bias the reporting of the results. If funding is present, the source—that is, journal article, news report, etc.—should include that information. When reading an article or listening to a report, the informationally literate person needs to consider if the funders had anything to gain by the results. If so, questions of validity and credibility in the findings may exist. Consider the findings of a study on a police-sponsored drug deterrence program where the employees of the program completed the data analysis and where the study was paid for using program funds. If the study results demonstrated that the program was not working, the program may not be funded again, and the employees would need to find another source of revenue or stop providing the program. If the funders did not have a stake in the results of the study, the funding will likely have less influenced the findings. A person evaluating the information for legitimacy should always contemplate the existence of funding.

4. **Can you trust the information from television, magazines, the Internet, and brochures?** Some reports in the media are based on peer-reviewed journal articles but some are not. Again, when hearing a report, one has to question where the information came from—the source—not who is reporting the information. Accordingly, a person should not just believe ABC News when they report record numbers in a motor vehicle thefts; instead, the individual should listen for the source of ABC News' information, which is hopefully the Federal Bureau of Investigation Uniform Crime Reports. The information literate person should also question if the information is consistent with previous information. For example, the media may claim that a finding is conclusive even though a single study's findings are never considered irrefutable, and other media outlets may be providing information contrary

to the news story. The information literate person must recognize that news stories focus on what is "new" and "exciting." Television stations need to sell advertising space to stay in business, and advertisers want to buy advertising space on television stations with the most viewers. The same goes for magazines and businesses who produce brochures. Funding may play a key role in the types of stories reported and/or the focus of the stories.

Thanks to President Trump, few people are not aware of the term *fake news*. Fake news seems to be all the buzz these days. Although it may not be a new trend, it has historically been used in news satire, the fact that the information shared in fake news is widely accepted as a reality is concerning. Fake news articles exist on the television, in magazines, and most popularly, on social media and the Internet. Fake news can include completely made-up stories that resemble credible journalism; stories that are only a little bit fake, such as stories that report actual truth but use distorted or decontextualized headlines to convince people to click on their web links; and news stories that are satirical or sarcastic (Hunt, 2016). Often times, the goal behind fake news on the Internet is to entice a reader to click on the story and visit a website to gain advertising revenue for the person hosting the website. According to a report in the *Guardian*, a man who was running a fake news website in Los Angeles told National Public Radio that he has made as much as $30,000 a month from advertising that rewards high traffic to his website (Hunt, 2016). Identifying fake news can be rather difficult, especially in criminal justice; however, the In the News 2.1 shows an example of fake news involving political fraud. The story was published on the Internet and spread through social media, reaching over 6.1 million people before it was discredited by Snopes.com (Garcia & Lear, 2016).

In the News 2.1

Thousands of Fake Ballot Slips Found Marked for Hillary Clinton

http://yournewswire.com/thousands-ballot-slips-hillary-clinton/

By Dmitry Baxter

Reports are emerging that "tens of thousands" of fraudulent ballot slips have been found in a downtown Columbus, Ohio, warehouse, and the votes are all pre-marked for Hillary Clinton and other Democratic Party candidates.

Randall Prince, a Columbus-area electrical worker, was performing routine checks of his companies wiring and electrical systems when he stumbled across approximately one dozen black, sealed ballot boxes filled with thousands of Franklin County votes for Hillary Clinton and other Democratic Party candidates.

"No one really goes in this building. It's mainly used for short-term storage by a commercial plumber," Prince said.

So when Prince, a Trump supporter, saw several black boxes in an otherwise empty room, he went to investigate. What he found could be evidence of an alleged election fraud operation designed to deliver Clinton the crucial swing state.

Early voting does not begin in Ohio until October 12, so no votes have officially been cast in the Buckeye state. However, inside these boxes were, what one source described as, "potentially tens of thousands of votes" for Hillary Clinton.

An affiliate in Ohio passed along a replica of the documents found in the boxes:

OFFICIAL GENERAL ELECTION BALLOT

COS 14-E 01

A	Franklin County, Ohio	B	General Election	C	November 8, 2016

Instructions to Voter

- **To vote:** completely darken the oval (●) to the left of your choice.
- Note the permitted number of choices directly below the title of each candidate office. Do not mark the ballot for more choices than allowed. Vote either "Yes" or "No," or "For" or "Against," on any issue.
- If you mark the ballot for more choices than permitted, that contest or question will not be counted.
- **To vote for a write-in candidate:** completely darken the oval (●) to the left of the blank line and write in the candidate's name. Only votes cast for candidates who filed as write-in candidates can be counted.
- Do not write in a candidate's name if that person's name is already printed on the ballot for that same contest.
- **If you make a mistake or want to change your vote:** return your ballot to an election official and get a new ballot. You may ask for a new ballot up to two times.

For President and Vice President	For U.S. Senator	For Prosecuting Attorney
(Vote for not more than 1 pair)	(Vote for not more than 1)	(Vote for not more than 1)

For President and Vice President
(Vote for not more than 1 pair)

A vote for any candidates for President and Vice President shall be a vote for the electors of those candidates whose names have been certified to the Secretary of State.

○ For President **Jill Stein** For Vice President **Ajamu Baraka** Green

○ For President **Donald J. Trump** For Vice President **Michael R. Pence** Republican

● For President **Hillary Clinton** For Vice President **Tim Kaine** Democratic

○ For President **Richard Duncan** For Vice President **Ricky Johnson** Nonparty Candidates

For U.S. Senator
(Vote for not more than 1)

○ **Scott Rupert** Nonparty Candidate
● **Ted Strickland** Democratic
○ **Tom Connors** Nonparty Candidate
○ **Joseph R. DeMare** Green
○ **Rob Portman** Republican
○ _____ Write-In

For Representative to Congress (15th District)
(Vote for not more than 1)

● **Scott Wharton** Democratic
○ **Steve Stivers** Republican

For State Representative (18th District)
(Vote for not more than 1)

○ **Kristin Boggs** Democratic

For Prosecuting Attorney
(Vote for not more than 1)

○ **Bob Fitrakis** Green
● **Zach Klein** Democratic
○ **Ron O'Brien** Republican

For Clerk of the Court of Common Pleas
(Vote for not more than 1)

● **Maryellen O'Shaughnessy** Democratic
○ **Besa Sharrah** Republican

For Sheriff
(Vote for not more than 1)

● **Dallas L. Baldwin** Democratic

For County Recorder
(Vote for not more than 1)

○ **Daphne Hawk** Republican
● **Danny O'Connor** Democratic

For County Treasurer
(Vote for not more than 1)

○ **Ted A. Berry** Republican

It is important to note that the above replica coincides with a ballot that a Franklin County voter would cast at the polling place on Election Day, meaning the Clinton campaign's likely goal was to slip the fake ballot boxes in with the real ballot boxes when they went to official election judges on November 8th.

Ohio, a perennial swing state in the presidential election, has been a challenge for Clinton and her Democrat counterparts in 2016. Many national Democrat groups have pulled funding from the state entirely, in order to redirect it to places in which they are doing better.

Clinton herself has spent less time in Ohio, and spent less money, in recent weeks as it has appeared that Trump will carry the crucial state.

With this find, however, it now appears that Clinton and the Democrat Party planned on stealing the state on Election Day, making any campaigning there now a waste of time.

This story is still developing, and more news will be published when we have it.

Spotting fake news and evaluating it is not easy because society is flooded with news stories all day, every day. Taking the time to assess and evaluate each one may be an impossibility. However, the information literate individual can rely on the skills he or she has learned to evaluate information to spot fake news. He or she can also look for fake news indicators, such as websites with red flags in their names like ".com.co" and by looking at a website's "About Us" page to determine the website's sources. The individual can use Google Chrome plugins to filter fake news articles from their Internet searches, and they can google the sources of any quotes or figures in articles he or she may read on the Internet or on social media. Additionally, the information literate person should question websites that he or she has never heard of before. Obscure websites or websites that end in ".org" may have an agenda behind their reporting practices (Hunt, 2016). Finally, using websites to fact check an article, like Snopes.com, which is a fact-checking website with more than 20 years of information, may help to evaluate the credibility of the information provided.

The authors of this book would be remiss if we did not mention that students should be cautious when using the Internet for research and information gathering in the first place. Libraries, both electronic and brick-and-mortar, are still the best and most consistent places to find legitimate information. Even though the Internet provides a plethora of information, not all of it is reliable. Anyone can publish anything they want (as long as it is not illegal) on the Internet, even going so far as to make the website where the information is published look genuine. Unlike journal articles that may undergo peer review, websites are not monitored for quality, accuracy, or bias. A popular example of this is Wikipedia.org. Students often refer to and cite Wikipedia in research papers, and Wikipedia claims to be an encyclopedia. Yet, Wikipedia is an information website with an "openly editable content" (Wikipedia: About, 2018, para. 1). Anyone with access to the Internet can modify a page on the Wikipedia.com website, and anonymous contributors edit most of the content on the website. Although Wikipedia.org contends that the information contributed must be verifiable and come from a reliable source, anyone can post information on Wikipedia.org about a topic whether he or she knows anything about the topic or not (Wikipedia: About, 2018, para. 4). Thus, it is especially important that the information literate person evaluate or use critical thinking skills to assess the resource closely on Wikipedia and all other websites.

When evaluating websites, individuals should consider whether the name of the author or creator of the information is published on the website. He or she should also consider the author or creator's credentials. Asking questions about the author or creator's occupation, experience with the subject matter, position, or education is crucial. Additionally, the informationally literate person should determine if the author is qualified to write about the topic and if there is contact information for the author or creator somewhere on the website. Another factor to consider is if the author or creator is writing for or associated with an organization. In other words, could their role in the organization potentially influence what is published on the website? The reader may also want to take into account the URL identification and domain name. Domain names with ".org" indicate an affiliation with an organization, while ".com" and ".biz" may be commercial or for-profit websites. Domain names like ".edu" and ".gov" commonly publish articles that have undergone review and may be scientific in nature, although it is still the reader's responsibility to determine their legitimacy by considering the other features of the website.

Although using a search engine, like Google, Yahoo, Bing, or Ask, is a simple way to find websites and articles on a topic, the information literate person has to comb through the web links provided using the factors discussed above to identify those that are most beneficial and valid. Aside from the random Internet websites that may appear in a web search, there are collections of works on search engines, like Google Scholar, where the information literate person can identify scholarly articles from a number of disciplines. Most of the articles on Google Scholar are peer reviewed and provide the author's name, citation, and location where the article is published. Google Scholar regularly provides links to libraries or websites on the Internet where students can find additional scholarly articles on the topic. Regardless of the type of Internet resource an information literate person chooses to use, asking questions about the purpose, objectivity, accuracy, reliability, credibility, and currency of each website is key to identifying appropriate information (Georgetown University Library, 2018).

Finally, it is during the evaluation process that information is deemed relevant, not relevant, or invalid. This is where critical thinking skills are most important, as the individual analyzes and assesses each piece of information. Relevant information is kept for future use while the information literate person dismisses information considered not relevant or invalid. The person then moves into the final phase of the process—*using the information effectively, ethically, and legally.*

Use the Information Effectively, Ethically, and Legally

Once the information literate person identifies the new information, he or she will consider it in combination with prior information and use all of the information to effectively resolve a problem or issue. In using the information, the individual will organize the information and present it in a way that provides a resolution to the problem or issue. The information literate person may write a paper or proposal or do a presentation to an interested audience. The information literate person may also create or implement policy or use the information for their personal lifestyle or work changes. In whatever way the individual uses the information, he or she should strive to share it with an audience through technology or personal communication.

The information acquired should also be used ethically and legally. This requires the informationally literate person to understand the ethical, legal, and socio-economic issues involved with the information and the medium in which it is shared. Issues such as privacy and security in printing, posting, or broadcasting should be considered. The individual should also consider censorship and freedom of speech issues as well as copyright and fair use laws (The Association of College and Research Libraries, 2000).

Copyright laws protect original works of authorship to include literary, dramatic, musical, and artistic works, as well as computer software and architecture. Copyright laws do not protect ideas, facts, systems, or methods of operations; however, the way these are extracted may be protected

(U.S. Copyright Office, n.d.). To ethically use information and under copyright laws, individuals are required to provide credit to the original authors of works when using a protected work. If they do not and the originator finds out, he or she can sue the person who used the work without credit or permission. Fair use laws are a clause in the copyright laws that allow nonprofit and educational institutions and libraries to reproduce works from original authors, prepare derivative works from the original works, and distribute copies of original works by sale or lease or other means. These entities can also perform the work publicly to include digital audio transmission and to display the copyrighted work (U.S. Copyright Office, n.d.). Although specific guidelines are attached to fair use, like the inability to photocopy textbooks or distribute copyrighted information to others, providing commentary, criticism, news reporting, and using copyrighted material in research and scholarship is allowable (when credit is provided to the original author). Individuals can also ethically and legally use information in the public domain. Although many believe that all of the information found on the Internet is public domain, this is not true. Works that fall within the public domain include those in which the intellectual property rights have expired, been forfeited, been waived, or where they do not apply. U.S. government documents are excluded from copyright law and are considered public domain. All other works, even those found on the Internet, are the intellectual property of the person who created them and fall within copyright-protected statutes. Informationally literate individuals must be diligent in their understanding of how information falls within copyright, fair use, and public domain regulations. These parameters are country based and can vary—meaning what is copyrighted in one country may be public domain in another (U.S. Copyright Office, n.d.). As such, providing credit to the originator or gaining permission to use the work is always the safest approach. The Digital Copyright Slider (2012) created by Michael Brewer and the American Library Association Office for Information Technology Policy is a practical guide for determining copyright, fair use, and public domain.

Developing information literacy skills takes time and effort. Information literate individuals practice the skills by becoming better and more efficient at locating, analyzing, and using the information. Often this practice requires the person to use technology in the process. Thus, he or she develops digital literacy, computer literacy, and technology literacy skills in addition to information literacy skills.

Exercise 2.1

You are a police officer. You receive a call about a domestic disturbance at a home on the south side of town. As you arrive at the home, you see two adults and four children standing in the yard. There are also three neighbors standing in the street. You know that you must use information literacy skills to determine what to do in the current situation. Using each of the skills identified in the chapter—know there is a problem, locate information, evaluate information, use and share the information—explain what steps you will take to resolve the domestic issue.

Digital Literacy, Computer Literacy, and Technology Literacy Skills

The information literate person will develop digital, computer, and technology literacy skills as he or she investigates topics using information literacy. These skills will likely become more effective over time and will greatly assist in gathering and dispersing information. Developing these skills allows collaboration with individuals near and far and dissemination of information beyond the intended audiences. As such, these skills, like being informationally literate, should be used within ethical and legal guidelines, namely privacy, copyright, confidentiality, and authorship.

Digital literacy is the "ability to use information and communication technologies to find, evaluate, create, and communicate information, requiring both cognitive and technical skills" (American Library Association, 2018, para. 2). Digital literacy includes reading digital content and using digital formats to find and create content. For example, reading a book on a Kindle is digital literacy, as is using a search engine to find an article on racial profiling and sharing the results of a police/citizen video with friends and family on social media. Another example is sending an email or tweeting about a weekend activity.

Digital literacy includes digital writing, which may involve emailing, blogging, tweeting, and so on. Digital writing is intended to be shared with others, so understanding its role in the social, legal, and economic community is important. Digital writing can be a potentially precarious tool if the information literate person does not consider the privacy implications of what he or she creates and shares and/or the safety and legal implications of sharing the information (Heitin, 2016). Consider an example where a 13-year-old female takes a picture of her genitals and Snapchats it to a boyfriend. If the boyfriend saves the photo and sends it to other friends, he may face criminal charges for distributing child pornography. By receiving the picture, he may also face criminal charges if he fails to report the photo to the proper adult or authority. The girl may face criminal charges for distributing child pornography. In this scenario, the picture may travel phone-to-phone through many youth, each facing their own privacy and legal issues when they receive, open, view, and, possibly, share the photo. The moral here is there is an increased responsibility that comes with digital writing and literacy that may not be as pressing in print writing. Print writing, depending on the source, customarily undergoes review before being disseminated, whereas digital information may not.

Computer literacy means that an individual has the basic knowledge and skills to use a computer. The person may be familiar with turning the computer on and off, word processing, printing documents, and so on. As the individual uses the computer, he or she may become even more literate in using other types of programs, operating systems, software applications, and web design. Computer literacy

> can be understood in the same way that traditional literacy applies to print media. However, because computers are much more advanced than print media in terms of access, operation and overall

use, computer literacy includes many more types of cognitive and technical skills, from understanding text and visual symbols, to turning devices on and off or accessing parts of an operating system through menus. (technopedia.com, 2018, para. 2)

Being able to code, develop web pages, and manage a network are higher-level skills developed by some computer literate individuals. Although not everyone will develop computer literacy skills comparable to a technical support assistant, most information literate individuals develop enough skills to surf the web, identify sources, develop documents and presentations, and disseminate information through the appropriate computer venues. For example, a police officer presenting training on gang identification may develop a PowerPoint presentation. A web technician employed by a state police department to maintain the department's website may post updated arrest statistics, mission statements, and pictures of police officers on patrol.

There are individuals who develop computer literacy skills but use them for illegal activity. They may create viruses, hack websites, and send out bogus or scam emails. The AARP reported in a survey of more than 11,000 Internet users that two-thirds received spam emails at least once per year (Paulas, 2016). Less computer literate individuals may fall prey to these phishing emails, especially if they closely mimic bank websites or formal notices from other businesses. Although the police and other social service agencies provide notices when illegal computer activity is flourishing in a specific geographical location, they cannot protect everyone from unethical computer practices. Classes designed to train people in computer literacy can be used to lower the potential for computer victimization, but these often require having discretionary money to pay for the classes. This is something some individuals may not find affordable. The information and computer literate individual will learn over time how to identify and avoid harmful computer practices and will observe legal standards when using the computer.

Exercise 2.2

Using a newspaper or media source, identify a recent virus or technological issue affecting Internet users.

Quite simply, technology literacy is the ability to use the appropriate technology to communicate and search for information. In technology literacy, a person knows when to use the Internet versus email or when to create a webpage versus a PowerPoint presentation. A crime analyst, for example, would know when to use an Excel spreadsheet to disseminate crime information instead of using SPSS, a statistical analysis software package. Developing technology literacy skills is ongoing process, as instructional and communications technologies change with every new invention. Computers and email are just the tip of the iceberg, as there now exist digitized kitchen appliances, self-driving vehicles, and integrated manufacturing. Who knows what the future holds with regard to technology. Regardless, most agree that technology literacy incorporates four basic skills: (1) the ability to adapt to rapid and continuous technology change; (2) the ability to develop creative solutions to technological problems; (3) the ability to process technological knowledge effectively, efficiently, and ethically; and (4) the ability to assess technology's place in social, cultural, economic, and legal environments (Wonacott, 2001). Developing and using these skills in conjunction with information literacy is vital to identifying information and using it to solve problems. It is also essential to workplace productivity, decision making, global integration, and on a more micro level, to finding and keeping a job.

In summary, the information literate person who develops digital, computer, and technology literacy is more likely to continue learning and developing new and better critical thinking skills. Additionally, they are likely to display other skills desired in the workplace, such as evaluation skills, analytical thinking, creativity, problem-solving, and research analysis and design skills. The literate person will demonstrate effective skills in decision making, such as acting in moral and ethical ways, and exercise more autonomy and positive work habits (Wonacott, 2001). Each of these skills is essential in the field of criminal justice.

CHAPTER SUMMARY

Information literacy is an acquired skill that allows individuals to know that they need information and to locate, evaluate, use, and share information. Information literacy is usually used to solve problems. Information literate individuals may use a variety of methods to find information, including media, print, the Internet, and other forms of technology. When doing so, the information literate individual is also developing skills in digital, computer, and technology literacy. All forms of literacy discussed in this chapter should be used within ethical and legal considerations. Knowing how the information a person disseminates can affect the social, cultural, economic, and legal environments is especially important in a global society.

Information literate individuals have better chances to acquire and keep jobs. They are more likely to display the types of skills employers demand, including critical thinking, evaluation, creativity, higher morals and ethics, and problem-solving abilities, among others. Workplace productivity can be greatly improved when organizations hire information literate persons. In criminal justice, being able to acquire, evaluate, use, and share information is an essential skill applied in every position and within all cases and interactions. When criminal justice professionals are not adept at information literacy, they can ruin cases, cause appeals, and in general, prevent the system from functioning effectively.

QUESTIONS FOR CONSIDERATION

1. How might a police officer use technology literacy to do his or her job?

2. Your college professor assigns you a paper for a class project. Using information, digital, computer, and technology literacy, explain how you would complete the project.

3. What ethical issues might an individual who posts information on social media face? What about legal issues? Provide an example post and discuss both the ethical and legal issues.

CHAPTER 3

Police Report Writing

The Face Page

Every police report includes a front or "face" page, which may include a section for writing a narrative or may require a separate page for the narrative section. The face page contains blocks where the officer enters basic information, such as the incident date, time, and location; the names and biographical information of a victim, witness, or suspect; the type of crime committed and the corresponding state statute number; and more. The information reported on the face page, though, is useful far beyond its application to the police investigation. This information is translated into data that are used by crime analysts, police managers, researchers, and criminal justice students to study national trends in crime. This chapter introduces students to the most common types of information reported on a face page, the uses for that data, and writing the report narrative.

Officers are required to write many different types of narrative documents. In policing, the basic incident report documents the officer's activity; records the actions and testimony of victims, suspects, and witnesses; serves as a legal account of an event; and is used for court testimony. As a professional, an officer should strive to become the best writer possible.

The need to write well has never been more important. Relating facts about an incident and investigation go far beyond the eyes of the supervisor and agency. Writing in general and writing well is a cornerstone of professional communication skills, and according to Lentz (2013) "is seen as a mark of professionalism and intelligence" (p. 475). Writing well is a necessary requirement in policing, and police officers are often expected to complete a variety of writing assignments. A well-written police report will convict criminals, encourage the support of the community, and become a guide by which the public and the courts will measure their respect for both the officer and department.

Additionally, police reports are public record in many states. As such, they are available for all to review. Attorneys, paralegals, and staff personnel on both sides of a case, as well as judges and journalists may read an officer's reports. Imagine a report being read by a Justice of the Supreme Court!

This chapter introduces students to the most common information reported on a face page and the uses for that data as well as information on writing the report narrative.

Common Data Fields

The specific data reported on the face page varies by individual agencies according to local needs and compliance with Uniform Crime Reporting program (UCR) and National Incident-Based Reporting System (NIBRS) reporting requirements. According to NIBRS policies, every incident report must contain, at a minimum, the following segments: administrative, offense, property, victim, offender, and arrestee (FBI, n.d.c, p. 64).

The Administrative Segment contains information that applies to the entire incident. The police agency will generate a case number for all incident reports. The case number is reported on the initial incident report and all supplemental and investigative reports. All documents related to an incident will share the same agency case number. The date, time, and specific location of the offense are also reported in this segment (FBI, n.d.c, p. 65).

Offense Segment

The criminal offense title, such as burglary or robbery, and the corresponding state statute are reported in this segment, unless the case is civil or non-criminal. If the incident involved more than one offense, each additional offense should be listed as well (FBI, n.d.c, p. 65).

Property Segment

This segment includes a list of each item of property that is damaged, destroyed, recovered, seized, or stolen. The list should include a description of each property item and its value. In the case of drug seizures, the quantity and estimated street value should also be included (FBI, n.d.c, p. 65). Property items listed on the incident report face page are generally limited to less than 10 items reported as being stolen or missing.

Property items reported as stolen by a victim should be described and valued according to the victim's testimony. Items that have been found by an officer or stolen items that have been recovered will also be reported in this section of the report. Officers should be particularly cautious when describing jewelry and drug items if they are not trained and qualified to accurately identify precious metals, gemstones, street drugs, and pharmacological drugs. A gold ring may bear a stamp indicating 24k gold, a presumptive drug test may give a positive result for cocaine, and a pill may appear in the *Physician's Desk Reference*, but without the proper training and instruments, officers often cannot state with certainty that many items are, in fact, what they appear to be. A more detailed discussion on recording property items appears in Chapter 6 of this text.

If a vehicle is involved in a case, as much detailed information as possible is reported on the face page. This information includes make, model, year, and color. Any distinguishing characteristics, such as body damage and missing parts, should be noted. One of the authors once identified and arrested a bank robbery suspect after a bumper sticker described by a witness was observed on a vehicle the day after the robbery. Finally, if available, officers should note the vehicle identification number (VIN) and license plate state and number. If the vehicle has been stolen, this information may be located on the vehicle title, registration, and insurance documents. The VIN can be located in places on the vehicle. See Image 3.1, Where to Locate Your VIN.

The VIN can often be found on the lower-left corner of the dashboard, in front of the steering wheel. You can read the number by looking through the windshield. The VIN may also appear in a number of other locations:

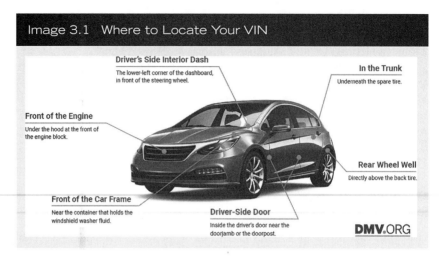

Image 3.1 Where to Locate Your VIN

Driver's Side Interior Dash
The lower-left corner of the dashboard, in front of the steering wheel.

In the Trunk
Underneath the spare tire.

Front of the Engine
Under the hood at the front of the engine block.

Rear Wheel Well
Directly above the back tire.

Front of the Car Frame
Near the container that holds the windshield washer fluid.

Driver-Side Door
Inside the driver's door near the doorjamb or the doorpost.

DMV.ORG

Source: dmv.org

- **Front of the engine block**. This should be easy to spot by popping open the hood and looking at the front of the engine.

- **Front of the car frame**, near the container that holds windshield washer fluid.

- **Rear wheel well**. Try looking up, directly above the tire.

- **Inside the driver-side door jamb**. Open the door and look underneath where the side-view mirror would be located if the door was shut.

- **Driver-side doorpost**. Open the door and look near the spot where the door latches, not too far from the seatbelt return.

- **Underneath the spare tire**.

Victim, Offender, and Arrestee Segments

These segments include information about the people involved in an incident, including the victim, witness, offender, and arrestee. The name, biographical information, address, and contact information is reported for the victim and witness. As much information as is known about an offender should also be listed, including race, sex, height, weight, hair and eye color, and any distinguishing scars, marks, or tattoos. Many times, the suspect is not known, but a description can be included. The arrestee segment includes the date of arrest and charge as well as the arrestee's age, race, and sex (FBI, n.d.c, p. 65).

Many times, the person who reports the incident is also the victim, and there are no other persons involved. But in more involved cases and lengthy investigations, the list of persons can grow quite long. Additional persons may include several victims and witnesses, back-up officers and case investigators, medical personnel, transportation personnel, crime scene technicians, investigators, and more. Officers should be diligent in identifying and reporting the information of those involved since prosecutors may find their testimony valuable during trial.

Two areas that deserve particular attention include race and sex. The modern changes to the definitions of racial and sexual identity can easily lead to errors in reporting this critical information. When completing the face page, officers should follow the Federal Bureau of Investigation (FBI) guidelines listed in Figures 3.1 and 3.2 when reporting the race and sex of persons involved in an incident.

Figure 3.1 FBI Race Codes

External Code	Literal	Description (If Subject Is)
A	Asian or Pacific Islander	Chinese, Japanese, Filipino, Korean, Polynesian, Indian, Indonesian, Asian Indian, Samoan, or other Pacific Islander
B	Black	A person having origins in any of the black racial groups of Africa
I	American Indian or Alaskan Native	American Indian, Eskimo, or Alaskan Native, or a person having origins in any of the 48 contiguous states of the United States or Alaska who maintains cultural identification through tribal affiliation or community recognition
U	Unknown	Of indeterminable race
W	White	Caucasian, Mexican, Puerto Rican, Cuban, Central or South American, or other Spanish culture or origin, regardless of race

Source: The Guidelines for Preparation of Fingerprints Cards and Associated Criminal History Information, Federal Bureau of Investigation.

Figure 3.2 FBI Sex Codes

External Code	Literal	Description
F	Female	Female
G	Female	Female Print, Male Reference
M	Male	Male
N	Male	Male Print, Female Reference
Y	Male	Male, Unreported
Z	Female	Female, Unreported
X	Unknown	Unknown Sex

Source: The Guidelines for Preparation of Fingerprints Cards and Associated Criminal History Information, Federal Bureau of Investigation.

Figure 3.3 Sample Incident Report Face Page

OFFENSE/INCIDENT REPORT
INSTRUCTIONS ARE PRINTED SEPARATELY. IF ADDITIONAL SPACE IS NEEDED, USE REVERSE OF FORM; IDENTIFY ITEMS.

1. TYPE		
☐ a. ORIGINAL	☐ b. CONTINUATION	☐ c. SUPPLEMENT OR FOLLOWUP

2. CODE NO.	2a. SORT	3. TYPE OF OFFENSE OR INCIDENT	4. CASE CONTROL NUMBER

5. BUILDING NUMBER	6. ADDRESS

7. NAME OF AGENCY/BUREAU	8. AGENCY/BUREAU CODE	9. SPECIFIC LOCATION	10. LOCATION CODE

11a. DATE OF OFFENSE/INCIDENT	11a. TIME OF OFFENSE/INCIDENT	12. DAY	13a. DATE REPORTED	13b. TIME REPORTED	14. DAY

15. JURISDICTION (X)	16. NO. OF DEMONSTRATORS	17. NO. EVACUATED	a. TIME START	b. TIME END
☐ EXCLUSIVE ☐ CONCURRENT ☐ PARTIAL ☐ PROPRIETARY				

18. PERSONS INVOLVED

ID CODE (a)	NAME AND ADDRESS (b)	AGE (c)	SEX (d)	RACE (e)	INJURY CODE (f)	TELEPHONE (g)
	Last Name, First, Middle Initial					HOME
	Number, Street, Apt. No., City and State					BUSINESS
	Last Name, First, Middle Initial					HOME
	Number, Street, Apt. No., City and State					BUSINESS

19. VEHICLE

a. STATUS

b. YEAR	c. MAKE	d. MODEL	e. COLOR (Top/Bottom)	f. IDENTIFYING CHARACTERISTICS

STOLEN	SUSPECT	g. REGIS-TRATION	YEAR	STATE	TAG NO.	h. VIN	i. VALUE
GOV'T.	PERSONAL						
VANDALIZED	RECOVERED						

20. ITEMS TAKEN

a. NAME OF ITEM	b. QUANTITY	c. OWNERSHIP ☐ GOV'T ☐ PERSONAL	d. BRAND NAME
e. SERIAL NO.		f. COLOR	g. MODEL

h. VALUE	i. UNUSUAL OR UNIQUE FEATURES

j. PROPERTY WAS ☐ SECURED ☐ UNSECURED	k. STATUS OF PROPERTY ☐ RECOVERED ☐ MISSING ☐ PARTIAL RECOVERY	VALUE RECOVERED

l. NAME OF ITEM	m. QUANTITY	n. OWNERSHIP ☐ GOV'T ☐ PERSONAL	o. BRAND NAME
p. SERIAL NO.		q. COLOR	r. MODEL

s. VALUE	t. UNUSUAL OR UNIQUE FEATURES

u. PROPERTY WAS ☐ SECURED ☐ UNSECURED	v. STATUS OF PROPERTY ☐ RECOVERED ☐ MISSING ☐ PARTIAL RECOVERY	VALUE RECOVERED

21. NARRATIVE (If additional space is needed, use blank sheet and attach.)

GENERAL SERVICES ADMINISTRATION

GSA FORM **3155** (REV. 3/2000)

Source: https://www.charleston-sc.gov/index.aspx? NID=631.

Figure 3.4 Sample 2 Incident Report Face Page

OHIO UNIFORM INCIDENT REPORT

ADMINISTRATIVE

AGENCY NAME

CALL NUMBER | *GEOCODE

TOD

TOA
- ☐ INCIDENT (NON-CRIMINAL)
- ☐ OFFENSE
- ☐ SUPPLEMENT

TOC

*INCIDENT NUMBER

*CLEARANCES

A ☐ Death of Suspect		G ☐	Arrest – Juvenile
B ☐ Prosecution Declined		H ☐	Warrant Issued
C ☐ In Custody of Other Jurisd.		I ☐	Invest. Pending
D ☐ Victim Refused to Coop.		J ☐	Closed
E ☐ Juvenile/No Custody		K ☐	Unfounded
F ☐ Arrest - Adult		U ☐	Unknown

*CLEARANCE DATE: | CLEARED BY:

*REPORT DATE/TIME				*INCIDENT OCCURRED FROM				*INCIDENT OCCURRED TO			
MONTH	DAY	YEAR	TIME	MONTH	DAY	YEAR	TIME	MONTH	DAY	YEAR	TIME

INCIDENT LOCATION (Street, Apt., City, State, Zip)

OFFENSE

*OFFENSE	*OFFENSE CODE	*A/C	F/M & DEGREE	*HATE/BIAS	*LARCENY	*TYPE CRIMINAL ACTIVITY
1.	1.					1.____ 2.____ 3.____
2.	2.					1.____ 2.____ 3.____
3.	3.					1.____ 2.____ 3.____
4.	4.					1.____ 2.____ 3.____
5.	5.					1.____ 2.____ 3.____

(Enter up to three for each offense)
- B- BUYING/RECEIVING
- C- CULTIVATING/MFG./PUB.
- D- DISTRIBUTING/SELLING
- E- EXPLOITING CHILDREN
- O- OPER/PROPOTING/ASSIST.
- P- POSSESSING/CONCEALING
- T- TRANSP/TRANSMITTING
- U- USING/CONSUMING
- G- OTHER GANG ACTIVITY
- J- JUVENILE GANG ACTIVITY
- N- NO GANG ACTIVITY

*LOCATION OF OFFENSE (Enter up to two)

1._____ 2._____

RESIDENTIAL STRUCTURE
01 Single Family Home
02 Multiple Dwelling
03 Residential Facility
04 Other Residential
05 Garage/Shed

PUBLIC ACCESS BLDGS.
06 Transit Facility
07 Government Office
08 School
09 College
67 Library
10 Church
11 Hospital

12 Jail/Prison
13 Parking Garage
14 Other Public Access Buildings

COMMERCIAL LOCATIONS
15 Auto Shop
16 Financial Institution
17 Barber/Beauty Shop
18 Hotel/Motel
19 Dry Cleaners/Laundry
20 Professional Office
21 Doctor's Office
22 Other Business Office
23 Recreation/Entertainment Center
54 Amusement Park
24 Rental Storage Facility
25 Other Commercial Service Loc.
56 ATM Machine Separate from Bank

59 Daycare Facility

RETAIL
26 Bar
27 Buy/Sell/Trade Shop
28 Restaurant
29 Gas Station
30 Auto Sales Lot
31 Jewelry Store
32 Clothing Store
33 Drugstore
34 Liquor Store
35 Shopping Mall
36 Sporting Goods
37 Grocery/Supermarket
38 Variety/Convenience
39 Department Store

40 Other Retail Store
41 Factory/Mill/Plant
42 Other Building

OUTSIDE
43 Yard
44 Construction Site
45 Lake/Waterway
46 Field/Woods
47 Street
48 Parking Lot
49 Park/Playground
50 Cemetery
51 Public Transit Vehicle
52 Other Outside Location
57 Camp/Campground
64 Rest Area

OTHER
53 Abandoned/ Condemned Structure
55 Arena/Stadium/ Fairgrounds/Coliseum
58 Cargo Container
60 Dock/Wharf/Freight/ Modal Terminal
61 Farm Facility
62 Gambling Facility/ Casino/Race Track
63 Military Installation
65 Shelter-Mission/ Homeless
66 Tribal Lands
77 Other

*SUSPECTED OF USING
- A ☐ ALCOHOL
- D ☐ DRUGS
- C ☐ COMPUTER EQUIPMENT
- N ☐ NOT APPLICABLE

*TYPE WEAPON/FORCE USED
1.____ 2.____ 3.____

METHOD OF ENTRY
- 1 ☐ FORCE
- 2 ☐ NO FORCE

*NO. PREMISES ENTERED

METHOD OF ENTRY – MOTOR VEHICLE THEFT
- 01 ☐ Motor Running/Keys in Car
- 02 ☐ Unlocked
- 03 ☐ Duplicate Key Used
- 04 ☐ Window Broken
- 05 ☐ Towed
- 06 ☐ Hot Wire
- 07 ☐ Slim Jim/Coat Hanger
- 08 ☐ Tumblers Removed
- 09 ☐ Column Peeled
- 10 ☐ Ignition Peeled

METHOD OF ENTRY – BURGLARY/B&E

ENTRY	EXIT		ENTRY	EXIT		ENTRY	EXIT
1 ☐ BASEMENT ☐		1 ☐ DOOR ☐			1 ☐ FRONT ☐		
2 ☐ 1ST FLOOR ☐		2 ☐ WINDOW ☐			2 ☐ SIDE ☐		
3 ☐ 2ND FLOOR ☐		3 ☐ GARAGE ☐			3 ☐ REAR ☐		
4 ☐ OTHER ☐		4 ☐ SKYLIGHT ☐			4 ☐ ROOF ☐		
		5 ☐ OTHER ☐			5 ☐ OTHER ☐		

METHODS OF OPERATION

*CARGO THEFT Y☐ N☐

VICTIM

*NO. | *TOTAL VICTIMS | *VICTIM TYPE | I ☐ INDIVIDUAL | F ☐ FINANCIAL INSTITUTION | P ☐ POLICE OFFICER (IN THE LINE OF DUTY) | S ☐ SOCIETY | O ☐ OTHER
B ☐ BUSINESS | G ☐ GOVERNMENT | R ☐ RELIGIOUS ORGANIZATION | U ☐ UNKNOWN

NAME (Last, First, Middle)

ADDRESS (Street, Apt., City, State, Zip) | PHONE

EMPLOYER NAME AND ADDRESS (Street, Apt., City, State, Zip) | PHONE

*AGE/ D.O.B. | *SEX | *RACE ☐ B ☐ A ☐ W ☐ I ☐ U | ETHNICITY | HGT | WGT | HAIR | EYES

OCCUPATION | SSN | *RESIDENT STATUS 1 ☐ RESIDENT 2 ☐ TOURIST 3 ☐ MILITARY 4 ☐ STUDENT 5 ☐ OTHER U ☐ UNKNOWN

*VICTIM INJURED? ☐ Y ☐ N | IF INJURED, DESCRIBE INJURIES:

*AGG. ASSAULT/ HOMICIDE CIRC. | TYPE OF ACT. | ASSIGN. TYPE | ORI – OTHER | *VICTIM/SUSPECT RELATIONSHIP 0.____ 1.____ 2.____ 3.____ 4.____ 5.____ | *VICTIM/OFFENSE LINK

*LEOKA INFORMATION

My signature verifies that the information on this report is accurate and true | DATE_____

INCIDENT NUMBER

REPORTING OFFICER | BADGE NO. | DATE

APPROVING OFFICER | BADGE NO. | DATE

FOLLOW-UP? ☐ Y ☐ N | If yes, follow-up Assignment:

ADDITIONAL SUPPLEMENTS
- ☐ VICTIM/WITNESS
- ☐ SUSPECT/ARRESTEE
- ☐ PROPERTY
- ☐ NARRATIVE
- ☐ STATEMENTS
- ☐ OTHER

FORM RECEIVED BY:
- ☐ INTELLIGENCE
- ☐ INVESTIGATION
- ☐ RECORDS

SPECIAL COPIES

8/2011

Source: https://www.femplate.com/forms-for-police/forms-for-police-3/.

Figure 3.3 (p. 40) is an example of an incident report form that includes a narrative section. This type of form could be used for simple reports, such as misdemeanors or incidents that did not involve contact with a suspect or injuries to those involved. Notice how this form is organized to capture the required UCR and NIBRS reporting requirement for administrative (blocks 1–17), property (blocks 15 and 20), victim, offender, and arrestee information (block 11).

Figure 3.4 (p. 41) is an example of a face page that does not include a section for the narrative. Notice the sections intended to collect the required UCR and NIBRS reporting requirement. Additionally, note the increased level of detail afforded by the removal of the narrative section. When this form is used, the narrative is placed on a separate page specifically designed for that purpose.

Uses of Face Page Data

The information contained in an incident report face page is useful for investigators, media outlets and the public, and national data reporting systems, such as the FBI's UCR and NIBRS. Investigators use face page data as the foundation for a criminal investigation. Information from each of the reporting segments is critical to an investigation and is often found in an investigator's follow-up report. Media outlets often create a police log from face page information that includes the type of offense; the date, time, and location of the offense; and the people involved in the incident. Face page information is important to the public to demonstrate proof of a loss for an insurance claim and learn about incidents that have occurred in their neighborhood or child's school. Accurate face page data are also important to the creation of national crime databases.

Uniform Crime Reporting and National Incident-Based Reporting System (NIBRS)

National crime data are compiled from the information reported by police officers on the incident report face page. Each month, the nation's city, university/college, county, state, tribal, and federal law enforcement agencies voluntarily submit crime data to the Federal Bureau of Administration (FBI). The FBI administers the UCR system and the NIBRS. These databases serve as the national repository for crime data submitted annually by almost 18,000 law enforcement agencies. Data from these programs are used to publish the annual *Crime in the United States* report, which includes "the volume and rate of violent and property crime offenses for the nation" (FBI, n.d.b) and the annual NIBRS report.

The UCR program was created in 1929 as a system of national crime statistics (FBI, n.d.a). The UCR has been in place for decades and collects data on eight offenses known to the police: criminal homicide, rape, robbery, aggravated assault, burglary, motor vehicle theft, other theft, and arson (U.S. Department of Justice, n.d.). Reid (1997), however, notes the reporting methodology used for the UCR has limitations. First, the UCR underestimates crime since it captures only crimes reported to the police, and many crimes go unreported (Reid, 1997). Second, the UCR uses a hierarchical system that captures only the most serious crime committed during a criminal event. If "a victim is raped, robbed, and murdered, only the murder is counted in the UCR" (Reid, 1997, p. 40).

Table 3.1 Uniform Crime Report, Crime in the United States

Year	Population	Violent crime	Violent crime rate	Murder and nonnegligent manslaughter	Murder and nonnegligent manslaughter rate	Rage (revised definition)	Rape (revised definition) rate	Rage (legacy definition)	Rape (legacy difinition) rate	Robbery	Robbery rate
2012	313,873,685	1,217,057	387.8	14,856	4.7			85,141	27.1	355,051	113.1
2013	316,497,531	1,168,298	369.1	14,319	4.5	113,695	35.9	82,109	25.9	345,093	109.0
2014	318,907,401	1,153,022	361.6	14,164	4.4	118,027	37.0	84,864	26.6	322,905	101.3
2015	320,896,618	1,199,310	373.7	15,883	4.9	126,134	39.3	91,261	28.4	328,109	102.2
2016	323,405,935	1,250,162	386.6	17,413	5.4	132,414	40.9	96,970	30.0	332,797	102.9
2017	325,719,178	1,247,321	382.9	17,284	5.3	135,755	41.7	99,856	30.7	319,356	98.0

In response to the limitations of the UCR, the NIBRS was first published by the FBI in 2011. The NIBRS was implemented to improve the quality and quantity of data collected by the police (FBI, n.d.b). The crime categories were expanded to 22 categories and take into account any relationship between the victim and offender as well as the use of drugs and weapons used (Reid, 1997).

Computerized Crime Mapping

While the narrative section of an incident report is valuable to investigators, the face page is particularly valuable to crime analysts. From this data, analysts can study the characteristics of crimes in order to identify patterns. With the use of computerized crime mapping, these analyses can then be used to locate crime hot spots and help administrators assign officers to the geographic locations where they are most needed. Computerized crime mapping, also known as geographic information systems (GIS), is the process of associating crime and the geography of an area to identify where, how, and why crime occurs (National Institute of Justice, 2013).

The location of crime and the local geography, including buildings, alleyways, and other prominent features of the cityscape, became an important focus of crime prevention theorists (Weisburd & Lum, 2005, p. 426). Using crime mapping, crime analysts can focus their attention on small geographical areas known as hot spots (Weisburd & Lum, 2005, p. 426). An example of a crime map can be seen in Figure 3.5.

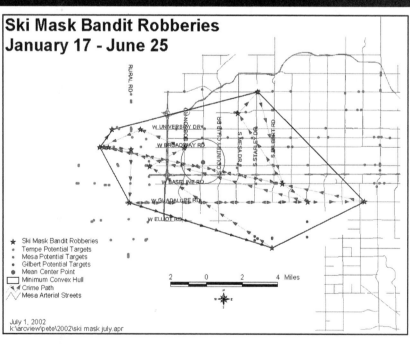

Figure 3.5   Example of a Crime Map

Source: Arizona Criminal Justice Commission, *Crime Mapping in Arizona Report*, 2002, p. 25.

In the News 3.1

Studies have demonstrated the effectiveness of the hot spot approach, and computerized crime mapping is viewed as an innovative and effective policing tool (Weisburd & Lum, 2005, p. 426). Reeves (2010) reported the majority of agencies serving a population of more than 25,000 used computerized crime mapping and that 100% of agencies serving populations of 250,000 or more used the technique (p. 22).

Tips for Writing the Incident Report
● ●

The need to write well in the criminal justice fields generally and in policing specifically has never been more important. Quible and Griffin (2007) observed that employers "consistently ranked oral and written education skills as among the most important, if not the most important, qualifications their employees should possess" (p. 32). Additionally, Kleckner and Marshall (2014) observed that "employers rated basic writing mechanics as second in importance among communication skills. . . . yet found that the employers' satisfaction level for this skill. . . . was the lowest among all communication skills" (p. 180). "Furthermore, the intangible costs of deficient writing include image degradation for both the employee and employer, reduced productivity when supervisors and officers must reread and correct poorly written reports, and incorrect decisions based on poorly written reports" (Quible & Griffin, 2007, p. 32). A well-written report will convict criminals, encourage community support, and reflect positively on the officer and the agency.

Basic Writing Skills

Like any skill, writing well requires practice and resources. First, one should obtain a useful, current writing style manual, like the one published by the American Psychological Association. Style manuals are easily found in local bookstores and online. Look for one that is fairly easy to use, and purchase the most recent edition available. An excellent online writing resource is the Purdue Online Writing Lab, https://owl.purdue.edu/owl/research_and_citation/apa_style/apa_formatting_and_style_guide/general_format.html. With some research, other online versions can also be found.

Computer spelling programs can be helpful when typing documents, but avoid becoming overly reliant and complacent since these programs will fail to indicate all errors. These programs will not detect improperly used homonyms, for example, such as there and their, here and hear, or too and two.

Writing for an Audience

Perhaps the most important concept in writing for the criminal justice professions is to always remember who will read the document—the audience. Of course, a supervisor and peers read the reports. Supervisors evaluate an officer's work, investigators use the reports as the foundation for an investigation, and the courts use reports to assess a defendant before and after trial. But a criminal justice document's audience does not stop there. As a public servant, a criminal justice professional's true audience is the citizens served.

Many criminal justice documents become public record, and as such, they are available for all to review. Attorneys, paralegals, and staff personnel on both sides of a case, as well as judges, may also read police reports. Imagine if a police officer writes a report being read by a Justice of the Supreme Court! Even today's cop crazy television shows are centered around police reports. It should go without question, then, that every report reflects the officer's best writing effort. Written reports are often the first indicator of professionalism to those who do not know a specific police officer, and sloppy reports give a bad impression. Every piece of writing should reflect the writer's best writing effort.

Writing Styles

The four academic writing styles include expository, narrative, descriptive, and persuasive. Briefly, the expository style explains a process, the narrative tells a story, the descriptive paints a picture for the audience, and the persuasive tries to convince the audience to agree with the writer's position on a topic. Although police reports are not academic writing assignments—nor should they be written or evaluated as such—officers use these writing styles in the narrative section of the incident report. Most often, the narrative of the police incident report requires a combination of narrative and descriptive writing styles. These styles are described in this section.

Narrative

The dominant writing style in a police report narrative is narration. Narratives tell a story by presenting events in an orderly structure and logical sequence (Kirszner & Mandell, 2010) that helps the reader understand the writer's purpose. Events are presented in chronological, or time, order beginning with the officer's initial involvement in an incident and ending when the officer concludes his or her role in the case so that readers will understand the sequence of events from beginning to end.

Descriptive

Descriptive writing is also appropriate for police reports, since these documents are required to be detailed and specific about names, times, dates, events, and geographic locations. Descriptive writing uses the five senses—sight, hearing, taste, touch, and smell—to tell the audience the physical nature of a person, place, or thing. In order for the narrative to be convincing, it must include specific details to help create a picture for the reader (Kirszner & Mandell, 2010). Police officers must describe with great detail and accuracy an incident or crime scene, observations of all types, and the result of criminal and what is often violent, graphic, and explicit behavior.

Source: https://www.cartoonstock.com/directory/c/chronological.asp

Eliminate Spelling Errors

Proper spelling is a vital part of every police report. Just as improper grammar and punctuation are a sign of semi-literacy, so too is improper spelling. A misspelled word screams for the reader's attention and shapes a negative image of the writer, supervisor, and the institution. Several misspelled words can have such a negative effect upon the reader that many will simply refuse to continue reading, finding it too difficult to understand the narrative. While a spell check will identify and correct misspelled words, it will fail to correct homophones. In this sentence, *four* example, the word "four" is misspelled, yet a spell check program would fail to identify the error.

The following (p. 48) is a list of the some of the most frequently misspelled words used in criminal justice writing.

Eliminate Slang and Jargon

Like any other professional, police officers develop a way of talking to other officers. The slang, jargon, and even 10-codes of the police profession have a way of creeping into reports and speech. This can lead to misinterpretation, though, for those who have no knowledge about the profession. At times, speaking in codes is an advantage, but report writing requires a communication style that conveys information to the reader clearly and concisely.

Below are some of the words most frequently used as police jargon. One can usually replace these words with simpler words that people without police experience easily understand. If an officer must use a slang or street term, immediately after using the term in the report, include an explanation for the reader. For example, an officer may write about items of contraband discovered during the search of a prisoner's cell like this: "I found a shank (common jail terminology for a homemade knife) hidden in the inmate's mattress."

Accept	Attack	Disturbance	Paraphernalia
Accurate	Attorney	Efficient	Receive
Accuse	Battery	Examination	Sergeant
Acquaintance	Bruise	Fellatio	Sheriff
Advisable	Bureau	Felony	Subpoena
Aggravated	Burglary	Foreign	Tattoo
Apparent	Canvassed	Harass	Trafficking
Appeal	Cemetery	Height	Trespass
Apprehend	Commit	Homicide	Trying
Apprehension	Conceal	Interrogate	Unnecessary
Approximate	Confidential	Intoxication	Vicinity
Argument	Conveyance	Jewelry	Victim
Armed robbery	Counsel	Judge	Warrant
Arraignment	Criminal	Lieutenant	Weight
Assault	Cunnilingus	Marijuana	Wounded
Associate	Discipline	Misdemeanor	

Table 3.2 Examples of Common Slang and Jargon Used in Incident Reports

Slang or Jargon	Reader Friendly	Slang or Jargon	Reader Friendly
Stated Verbalized related	Said	Altercation physical disturbance mutual combat struggle	Fight
Transpired	Happened	Closed fist open fist	Fist
Exited	Got out/left	Struck battered contacted	Hit
Responded to the area of	Went to (specific location)	Was in possession or possessed	Had
Initiated/instigated commenced	Started	Verbal altercation verbal dispute verbal confrontation	Argument
Attempted made an effort	Tried	Located/discovered	Found
Monitored surveilled	Watched	Observed viewed perceived	Saw

Remember, professional does not mean convoluted or fancy. Officers should write reports in general English that most people can easily understand. Examples of jargon are provided in Table 3.2.

Eliminate Emotion

In face-to-face conversation, emotional content is communicated through tone of voice, facial expression, and body language (Melé, 2009). In written documents, the writer expresses emotion through tone. According to Charles Baldick in the *Oxford Dictionary of Literary Terms* (1996), tone refers to the author's attitude toward the reader or subject matter. The tone of a narrative "affects the reader just as one's tone of voice affects the listener in everyday exchanges" (Ober, 1995). Writers of criminal justice narratives should strive for an overall tone that reflects an impartial, courteous, fair observer, that contains nondiscriminatory language and an appropriate level of difficulty for the audience (Ober, 1995).

Use a Professional Voice

Professional is a word with which many officers struggle. In the context of the written police report, a professional voice refers to the writer's tone and vocabulary. Officers should avoid writing like they talk, instead adopting a more professional voice appropriate for a business report. Professional writing is more structured than speech, uses longer sentences, and is more detailed than conversational speech, which relies on short, simple sentences and few details (as cited by Biber & Gray, 2010).

The writer's voice, though, should not attempt to impress readers with a large vocabulary or police jargon. An officer would do better to write a clear and easily readable report.

Answer the Interrogatives

Interrogatives introduce questions. They are the who, what, when, where, why, and how required in many criminal justice documents. The following is a partial list of basic interrogatives.

Who

1. Who is the victim, witness, suspect, defendant?
2. Who called the officer or reported the crime?
3. Who are the other officers who assisted your investigation?
4. Who are the medical personnel who treated any injuries?
5. Who discovered the event or crime?
6. Who was the first to arrive at the scene?
7. Who transported the injured to the hospital?
8. Who transported the defendant to medical?
9. Who discovered or recovered the evidence?
10. Who submitted the evidence for retention?
11. To whom was the evidence submitted?

12. Who photographed the crime scene?

13. Who signed the search/arrest warrant?

14. Who authorized the use of the technique/procedure?

15. Who were the backup officers?

16. Who comprised the entry team?

What

1. What is the incident?

2. What happened first?

3. What weapons or tools were used to facilitate the crime?

4. What involvement did the victim have in the incident? Was there any victim/perpetrator confrontation?

5. What happened next?

6. What drugs were used?

7. What name brand chemical presumptive test kit was used to test the drugs?

8. What injuries did the victim receive?

9. What treatment did the injured receive?

10. What observations did you make?

11. What action did you take?

12. What weapons did you use?

13. What questions did you ask the inmate?

14. What is the victim's relationship to the inmate?

15. What property was stolen?

16. What was the motive?

When

1. When did the incident occur?

2. When was the incident first discovered? Reported?

3. When was the incident first reported to institutional staff?

4. When did the officer arrive at the scene?

5. When was the evidence discovered?

6. When did the injured receive medical treatment?

7. When was the deceased pronounced dead?

8. When was the arrest made?

9. When was the property impounded/released?

10. When was the inmate interviewed?

11. When did the inmate confess?

12. When was the inmate advised of Miranda rights?

13. When was the stolen property recovered?

Where

1. Where did the incident take place?

2. Where was the inmate at the time of the crime or incident?

3. Where was the inmate found?

4. Where was the evidence found?

5. Where was the evidence submitted for retention/analysis?

6. Where were the witnesses in relation to the incident?

7. Where were the injured treated?

8. Where did the officer conduct any follow-up investigation?

9. Where was lighting located near the scene?

10. Where did the officer receive specialized training for the technique/ procedure used?

11. From where did the officer respond?

12. Where was the inmate transported?

13. Where was the inmate interviewed?

Why

1. Why did the crime occur? (motive)

2. Why did the inmate wait to report the crime?

3. Why did the inmate react the way they did?

4. Why did the officer respond the way he/she did?

5. Why did the inmate confess?

6. Why is the informant motivated to give information?

7. Why were weapons authorized to be used by officers?

8. Why did the criminal attempt succeed/fail?

9. Why were specialized units requested?

10. Why was the officer involved in the incident?

11. Why is the officer writing this report?

12. Why did the inmate resist restraint?

13. Why was the inmate involved in the crime?

14. Why was the officer in the area of the incident?

15. Why did the officer stop the inmate?

16. Why was the officer in fear?

17. Why did the officer detain the inmate?

18. Why did the officer release the inmate?

How

1. How did the incident occur?

2. How did the inmate gain entry/exit?

3. How was the incident discovered?

4. How was the property removed from the scene?

5. How was the incident reported?

6. How long did the incident last?

7. How was the inmate dressed?

8. How were weapons used?

9. How did the inmate defend himself or flee?

10. How did the officer respond to the inmate's requests for help?

11. How did the confrontation begin/end?

12. How was the inmate subdued/restrained?

13. How was the item removed?

14. How did the injury/death occur?

15. How many officers/units assisted in the investigation?

16. How much contraband was seized?

17. How much did the drugs weigh?

Take Good Notes

Proper note-taking skills are vital to the accuracy of initial and follow-up reports. Note taking is the process of gathering and recording facts and information relevant to an incident. Officers gather a variety of information in a quick and efficient manner, so they may recall the facts of the case to write the incident report, assist follow-up investigations, and refresh their memory for court testimony.

Police officers often use a small, pocket-sized writing pad for gathering initial notes. Some officers use a digital voice recorder to record notes, crime scene observations, and witness and victim statements.

In practice, field notes should be written in a standard format to record valuable information. The standard format helps officers later when called upon to recall information from on-scene notes. In on-scene notes, officers may make entries with symbols that only they understand and use flexible shorthand to quickly record data. This is perfectly acceptable because only the officer is required to interpret this information from the notes later.

Writing the Narrative

The narrative section of a police report tells a story. Like any other form of writing, the narrative must have a logical structure to help readers follow the line of reasoning and reach the same or similar conclusion held by the writer. The narrative should have a distinct beginning, middle, and end that consist of an introduction, a body, and a conclusion.

Writing a narrative requires more than just jotting down some information—it is a carefully crafted piece of persuasive writing. Of course, the narrative records data and facts relative to an incident. But it is important that the audience understands the facts of the case, the actions taken by officers, and how and why decisions were made. The narrative of the document must contain not only all of the vital case information, but it must also be logically constructed.

Criminal justice academic and professional narratives should follow a chronological order of events that have a distinct beginning (introduction), middle (body), and end (conclusion).

Narrative Structure

Introduction

The introduction in police incident reports is the first paragraph of the document. It is the reader's first exposure to the events about which the officer is writing. In a telephone conversation in which the parties have never met, the callers quickly reach conclusions about each other from voice, word choice, and conversational ability. Readers, too, will quickly form an opinion of the writer's competency as a writer, officer, and investigator from the first few sentences of the document. And this assumption goes well beyond the individual—an officer's reports also present the reader with an image of the criminal justice agency as a whole. Therefore, the officer is obligated personally and professionally to present to the audience the best possible impression. An officer creates this favorable impression not by using fancy words, slang, or jargon. The officer accomplishes a positive impression by presenting the reader with all of the necessary information in a clear and logically presented narrative. A writer should never assume the reader has the same knowledge about the case that he or she does. Therefore, a good introduction starts with a general statement about the case, gives any relevant background information, and focuses upon a thesis statement.

The Thesis Statement

A thesis statement is a clear and concise declaration of the main idea. In addition to helping the reader quickly and easily determine the writing purpose, it should also help the writer focus on the writing task. A clearly written thesis statement focuses the reader's attention upon the writer's topics. Examples:

1. At about 3:15 p.m. on 06/01/2018, I responded to cell 2015 when I heard an inmate screaming from inside the cell.

2. On 06/01/2018, while assigned to Pod B control, I saw a fight begin between several inmates in the Pod B common area.

Although some information, such as names, dates, times, and locations, may be contained in other areas of a document, officers must reintroduce that information in the narrative's introductory paragraph. The narrative should contain enough details so that it can stand alone without the support of information contained in other areas of the paperwork. This idea follows a key concept of this book—writing in a reader-friendly format that promotes communication and understanding. By reintroducing details, the writer helps the reader follow the narrative without having to leave the page and scan another section for pertinent information.

The Body

The separate paragraphs of the narrative's body should each focus upon a single idea or theme. For example, an officer might dedicate separate paragraphs to discuss an incident scene, a victim's statement, stolen property, or suspects.

A writer should use a topic sentence to focus the main idea of each paragraph. Like a thesis statement, the topic sentence helps both the reader and writer concentrate on what is to come. It is often the first sentence of the paragraph and presents the main idea of the paragraph ahead.

A good topic sentence is written clearly and concisely and identifies the subject or specific issue to be developed. Without some clearly stated direction, a reader is more likely to become confused about the writing. Just as a writer must present the total narrative in a clear and logical order, the writer must also do so within the paragraph. All of the parts of the document must be coherent and fit together so that it makes sense to the reader.

The structure of sentences within the paragraph can follow several models for a logical presentation. A writer can relate the events in chronological or time order as they happened. Or the writer might give special prominence to some event and leave the most important information for last. Relating the events as they occurred in a chronological, time-ordered fashion is often the simplest and easiest way to do this.

Conclusion

In the introductory paragraph, a writer would have told the reader what he or she intended to write with a thesis statement. Now, in the conclusion paragraph, the writer must remind the audience of what has been written. A writer can effectively do this by restating the thesis. Rather than simply writing the thesis statement again, though, a writer should retell it in a slightly different fashion. For example, a writer could restate the thesis statement from Example 1 above as follows:

My investigation concludes the screaming I heard was from Inmate Jones, Allen, who was being kicked and punched by Inmate Smith, Michael.

Formatting the Incident Report

The Beginning

Paragraph 1

Background information

a. Date

b. Time

c. Officers involved

d. Assigned location

e. Office building

f. Room or office number

g. Facility name

h. Type of call

The Middle

Paragraph 2

What happened when you arrived?

1. What did you see?

 a. Use descriptive language to paint an overall picture of scene.

2. How many subjects? (Use a separate paragraph to describe each subject.)

 a. A brief description of the subjects

 i. Gender

 ii. Race

 iii. Any blood or other evidence of injuries?

3. In a single sentence, what did the first reporter or witness tell you?

Paragraph 3

If needed, add additional paragraphs for each subject following the format for Paragraph 2.

Paragraph 4

Describe your sensory perception of the scene.

1. What did you hear?
   a. Arguing, talking
      i. What was the subject saying?
2. What did you see?
   a. Fighting or wrestling
      i. Describe in detail (punching, kicking, biting, throwing objects)
      ii. Drinking alcohol
      iii. Injuries
      iv. Evidence
      v. Other disruptive or illegal behavior
3. What did you smell?
   a. Alcohol
   b. Marijuana
   c. Urine or feces
   d. Decomposition
   e. Other odors
4. What did you touch?
   a. Items that were hot or cold
   b. Weather conditions (rain, snow, wind, etc.)
   c. Room temperature

Paragraph 5

What did you do?

1. Approach, detain, separate, interview subjects
2. Interviews
   a. Tell the subject's version of the event.
   b. What did witnesses tell you?
3. What did you do?
4. Call for assistance or supervisor?
5. Collect evidence?
   a. Photographs
   b. Other items of value

6. Paperwork

    a. Obtain sworn, written statements

    b. Witness statements

    c. Other official forms

7. Arrest information (if applicable)

    a. Name of official charge

    b. State statute number

    c. Who transported the subject to medical?

    d. How was the subject transported to medical?

The End

Paragraph 6

What did you do after the incident?

1. Submit evidence?

2. Make any notifications?

3. Any other official action that you took?

Table 3.3 Incident Report Writing Checklist				
Writing Process	**Organization**	**Format**	**General Writing**	**Grammar**
☐ Notetaking—gather the facts	☐ Use a distinct beginning, middle, and end	☐ 1st person	☐ Answer who, what, when where, why, how	☐ Use standard grammar
☐ Write the 1st draft	☐ Thesis statement	☐ Active voice	☐ Use names—not labels (victim, witness, suspect)	☐ No spelling errors
☐ Edit for grammar errors	☐ Each paragraph uses a topic sentence	☐ Past tense		☐ No punctuation errors
☐ Edit for writing errors	☐ Each paragraph focuses on a single idea	☐ Chronological order		☐ No abbreviations
☐ Edit for organization errors				☐ No sentence structure errors (fragments, run-ons, comma splices)
☐ Write the final draft				

Editing

There are three parts to the writing process—prewriting or planning, writing, and rewriting or editing. Every written document should be edited. Editing is often more than simply proofreading for basic errors. For many writers, editing involves major structural and thematic revisions.

This type of major writing surgery is very easy for officers who are fortunate enough to write criminal justice documents with a computer. Studies have found computer-aided writers make more changes to their work and revise at all stages of their writing (McAllister & Louth, 1988). Rather than waiting to revise until the project is completed, as do most hand writers, the computer-aided writer effectively revises while writing. Menu bar and function key options that aid editing and revision include spell check, grammar check, format, text insert and delete, and text scanning methods.

While many writers fear the blank page and find getting started difficult, the computer, with all its writer's aids, seems to invite writing since the text is manipulated on the screen before it even touches the page. And once the writer understands the function keys, moving through the text to revise becomes easier. Rather than writing and erasing or sometimes starting all over, as in a hand-written document, the insert, delete, and move text functions can make revision easier.

Those who write by hand can still effectively edit their work and submit well-written, organized, and error-free reports. Editing should be done at three levels to include word-level, sentence-level, and global revisions.

Word-Level Editing

A writer should never go to work without a bag of writing tools. Basic writing tools should include a dictionary (either a paperback version or an electronic model), a thesaurus, and this book or another grammar or writing handbook.

Even though a thesaurus is useful, a writer should be cautious when using one. A writer should not overly rely upon the thesaurus as a tool to eliminate repetition of key words or phrases in reports. While a thesaurus is a useful tool, it can, like anything else, be abused. An experienced reader will quickly spot dependence and view this as a weakness in word choice and writing skills.

Sentence-Level Editing

A writer should scan the document narrative quickly but thoroughly, paying particular attention to the sentence structure, such as run-ons, comma splices, and fragments. He or she should also consult a grammar book for questions concerning sentence structure, the use of commas, and other structural devices that may not be familiar. Effective writers often seek resources such as these to help correct and improve their writing.

Global Editing

Reread the narrative again; paying particular attention to structure and organization is imperative. The writer should ask if the incident report has a clear beginning, middle, and end. Is there a clear thesis statement in the introduction and a restatement of the thesis in the conclusion? Is the body logically structured, with each paragraph focusing on a single main topic? Is each paragraph focused and introduced by using a clearly written topic sentence? If not, the writer should make any necessary changes.

A writer should never write anything without first planning the structure of the work. The type of incident being documented will often dictate the structure of the report. Sometimes a writer will be able to decide what format to follow while, other times, he or she may not. The only rule to follow here is that the organization is logical and easy for readers to follow.

When editing for content, a writer should read the report first from beginning to end while asking himself or herself the six interrogative questions: who, what, when, where, why, and how. The writer should read quickly but efficiently to determine if he or she has answered everything that someone unfamiliar with the event would want to know. Is there anything more that could be added that would make the document more complete and easier to understand? Any omissions should be corrected at this point.

Table 3.4 Content Checklist: Be sure to include this information in the incident report

Incident	Inmate	Staff member	Infraction
Date and time	Name	Charging member name	Infraction code
Location	Identity number	Charging member job code	Infraction type
	Enemy level	Witness names	Infraction severity
	Inmate statement		Infraction narrative
	Inmate plea		
	Inmate demeanor		

Source: Adapted from Harrison, Weisman, & Zornado, 2017, p. 140.

In the News 3.2

Connecticut State Police Release New Report on Sandy Hook Shooting Response

By George Colli

Connecticut State Police released a report on the response to the 2012 Sandy Hook Elementary School that left 26 children and educators dead. A section of the report specifically addressed issues regarding late reports and the submission of reports that had errors despite having been approved by a supervisor. The report emphasized the importance of report writing competencies and the need to take immediate corrective steps to prevent inaccurate, untimely, and poorly written reports. Additionally, at the time of the incident certain units did not fully utilize the agency's electronic reporting system, which made it difficult for the assigned investigators to access and review reports.

CHAPTER SUMMARY

All incident reports include a "face page" or cover page. The face page consists of blank spaces and check boxes where the reporting officer enters information, such as the incident date, time, and location; the names and biographical information of a victim, witness, or suspect; the type of crime committed; and the corresponding state statute number. This information is commonly used for statistical analysis, crime mapping, and administrative analysis. The FBI also uses this data to compile the annual Crime in the United States and National Incident-Based Reporting System reports.

Writing well requires a process of planning, writing, and editing. Whether putting pen to paper or writing electronically, producing the best written work cannot be accomplished by simply writing alone. The written report is where an officer becomes a storyteller and engages the audience. The report should be written chronologically in narrative format to tell a story using descriptive words. Officers should follow general writing guidelines, eliminate slang and jargon and emotion, and answer all appropriate interrogatives. All writing must be written in standard English and error free. Finally, a well-written document requires editing. Writers should edit every written document at the word and sentence level as well as globally. Following these guidelines will help writers produce quality writing that reflects positively on themselves and the agency.

QUESTIONS FOR CONSIDERATION

1. List three uses for the data collected on the incident report face page.

2. How are data reported on the face page useful to crime analysts?

3. List some of the differences between the UCR report and the NIBRS.

4. Why is accurate data entry important to completing the face page of a police report?

Supplemental, Investigative, and Traffic Crash Reports

Many police investigations require that officers and investigators use particular reporting forms—either electronic or paper—in addition to an incident report form. These documents, like an incident report, often include a written narrative in which the officer tells a story of his or her involvement in an official event.

According to Reeves (2011), many officers use in-field computers to write and transmit their reports. A census of law enforcement agencies conducted in 2007 found that 90% of officers employed in larger agencies have access to in-field computers to access driver and vehicle records, criminal histories, and report writing software (Reeves, 2011). Smaller police agencies, though, may lack the funds to purchase computers and, therefore, require incident reports to be hand written.

This chapter examines the various police report forms that are often included as part of an initial or follow-up investigation.

Officers are required to use a variety of forms or electronic templates in order to thoroughly and accurately document information related to an incident. The incident report is the most common type of writing assignment in policing. The incident report form is used to document information when it is first reported to the police. It is usually written by a patrol officer to officially document a crime or other incident—reported by a citizen or when the officer makes an arrest. Many times, officers can effectively report an incident without the need for additional forms. In more complicated initial cases and investigations, the following additional forms are often used. This list is not intended to be definitive. Specific agencies and prosecutorial jurisdictions may require additional forms or documents.

Incident Report

The incident report is a common writing assignment in criminal justice professions and includes a narrative describing an incident. Although investigators are tasked with completing the investigation of crimes reported to the police, the investigation may reveal other crimes not initially reported. In these cases, many agencies require the investigator to complete an initial incident report to officially document the event.

The purpose of the narrative is to convey information to the audience in a clear, concise, and grammatically correct manner. It is the place where the writer becomes a storyteller and has the opportunity to relate the details of the investigation, observations, and actions. It is the most crucial and important part of any criminal justice document. Like any other form of writing, the narrative must have a logical structure to help readers follow the line of reasoning and reach the same or similar conclusion held by the writer. The narrative should have a distinct beginning, middle, and end that consist of an introduction, the body, and a conclusion. Writing a narrative requires more than just jotting down some information—it is a carefully crafted piece of persuasive writing. Of course, the narrative records data and facts relative to an incident. But it is important that the audience understands the facts of the case, the actions taken by officers, and how and why decisions were made.

Supplemental Reports or Follow-Up Report

The supplemental report is an addendum to the incident report. It is used "to keep the file current as new or corrected information is gathered" (Swanson, Chamelin, Territo, & Taylor, 2003, p. 168). The supplemental report is often used by officers and investigators to document information to the original incident report. In cases that require a lengthy narrative, the supplemental report form often serves as an extension of the incident report form narrative section. It can also be used by officers at the initial scene who assisted the case officer to document their role in the case. Additionally, investigators often use the supplemental report form to document their activities during an investigation. The supplemental report contains detailed information and is most often used to document interviews, evidence collected, or other activity related to a case that occurred after an officer's original incident report.

Evidence Report

It is common for officers to seize or collect physical items. These items are generally referred to as "property" and may or may not have evidentiary value. Property items can be almost anything of evidence or monetary value: contraband, found stolen items, any item that creates a link between a suspect and a crime, cash, drugs, firearms, and much more. Advances in the technology available to criminal justice agencies have expanded the scope of items of evidentiary value to include video and audio recorded on cell phones, body and in-car cameras, housing unit cameras located in adult and juvenile detention facilities, courtroom cameras, and surveillance cameras. The evidence report form is used to document any item that has been seized by an officer. It is a legal document that keeps a record of the collection, transportation, storage, chain of custody, and release of any item that comes into police custody. Seized items are stored in a secure evidence room until they can be legally returned to the owner, destroyed, or auctioned as unclaimed property.

Since physical evidence is often associated with investigating crimes, officers will find themselves collecting and recording the seizure of items on an evidence submission form. While the format and style of these forms will vary greatly from one agency to another, one similarity exists: officers must accurately describe any items that have been collected.

An accurate description of evidence is vital to the successful prosecution of a case. Officers must be detailed yet cautious in describing drugs, jewelry, money, and other valuables.

Drugs

Illegal and prescription drugs have become exceedingly popular and varied in today's society. As such, officers are often confronted with the task of describing pills, powders, capsules, and more. An officer may recognize commonly seized drugs such as cocaine or cannabis. These drugs are often quickly identified in the field with a chemical field presumption test kit. But for submission and description purposes, any account of these items should be purposely generic since a substance's identity cannot be certain without a lab or expert analysis. When describing drugs, officers should use the following terminology:

Drug Terminology

- Powder cocaine—unknown white powder, suspected cocaine

- Crack cocaine—unknown substance, suspected crack cocaine

- Cannabis—unknown green leafy substance, suspected cannabis

- Heroin—unknown (color) powder, suspected heroin

- Prescription pill or capsule—unknown (color) pill (list any markings such as manufacturer, numbers, and cross score)

Table 4.1 refers to commonly used names of street drugs.

Table 4.1	Commonly Abused Drug Street Names		
Drug Name	**Effect**	**Form**	**Street Name**
Ketamine	Hallucinogenic, depressant	Liquid	Special K
Methamphetamine	Stimulant	Powder	Crank, speed, chalk, fire
Crystal Methamphetamine	Stimulant	Chunks or small rocks	Ice
Heroin	Depressant	Powder	Antifreeze, big H, brown sugar, tar, junk
Cocaine	Stimulant	Powder	Dust, flake, powder, white, nose candy
Ecstasy or MDMA	Alters mood and perception	Tablet, capsule, liquid	E, Molly, essence, roll, Stacy
Gamma Hydroxybutrate (GHB)	Depressant	Liquid or powder	Liquid X, organic quaalude, scoop
Rohypnol	Date-rape drug, sedative, muscle relaxant	Oblong light green pill	Mexican valium, roofies, rope, forget-me pill

Adapted from Teen Drug Slang: Dictionary for Parents, WebMD, https://www.webmd.com/parenting/features/teen-drug-slang-dictionary-for-parents#2.

Money

On occasion, a police officer may confiscate money. Money must be counted accurately. All monies should be recounted several times with at least one other person present to verify the amount. In recording money on the evidence form, the officer should list the total amount, the nationality of the funds, and the number of each denomination. Then, immediately submit all cash to the agency evidence section to avoid any accusations of impropriety.

Example:

$1,000 United States currency in the following denominations: 5 $100, 4 $50, and 15 $20.

Jewelry

Like describing narcotics, the prevalence, variety, and value of jewelry demands caution when it comes time to list items on an evidence form. Jewelry manufacturers are particularly adept at creating imitation jewelry that appears surprisingly authentic. Some synthetic stones, in fact, cannot be distinguished from their authentic counterparts without the aid of a trained jeweler or gemologist.

Jewelry should be describe based on its appearance. When describing a woman's wedding band, for example, one should focus on the color and shape of the stone and ring rather than describing it as a diamond in a gold band. Officers should be equally cautious when describing items that carry a brand name since many counterfeiters have produced copies that are very difficult to distinguish from the real thing. A police officer is not a professional jeweler. Here are some suggestions for describing jewelry and watches.

Instead of "diamond ring," write the following:

1. One woman's ring with a gold-colored band containing a single, round, clear-colored stone.

2. One woman's ring with a silver-colored band and a single, round, clear-colored stone surrounded by eight smaller, round, blue-colored stones.

Instead of "Rolex watch," write the following:

1. One man's wristwatch with a round, blue-colored face and a silver- and gold-colored wristband.

2. One man's wristwatch with a square, tan-colored face and a wristband.

Instead of "gold chain," write the following:

1. A woman's neck chain, 18 inches long, gold colored.

2. A man's neck chain, 24 inches long, gold colored, with a round medallion, also gold colored.

Arrest Warrants

An arrest warrant is a written order, signed by a judge, based upon probable cause and particularly describing the person to be seized. A judge may issue an arrest warrant if probable cause exists to believe a defendant committed a criminal offense (Legal Information Institute, n.d.a).

The Fourth Amendment of the United States Constitution governs all that relates to the arrest warrants. The original 10 constitutional amendments, otherwise known as the Bill of Rights, were born in response to the actions of British King George III prior to the American Revolutionary War. The Bill of Rights sought to protect citizens against an over-zealous government. The Fourth Amendment specifically protects citizens against unreasonable searches and arrest. It safeguards citizen's homes, their property, and their person against unreasonable government actions by requiring an independent review of the facts by the court.

The Fourth Amendment requires that all arrest warrants be completed in writing. Most law enforcement agencies or prosecutor's offices will have a standard form required for use and require the arrest warrant to be supported by oath or affirmation before a judge. The judge issuing the warrant must have jurisdiction over the location of where the crime was committed and believe that the arrest is based upon probable cause. It is not only important for an officer to be able to articulate the specific probable cause related to the arrest warrant, but officers should also be able to clearly define probable cause during testimony. Failure to do so will help the defense in their attempt to discredit the officer. Probable cause is the facts of the case that would lead a reasonable officer to believe that a crime has been or is about to be committed. The person to be arrested must be described in a way that is sufficiently clear so that he or she can be easily identified as the proper person to be arrested. Finally, the seized person must be brought before the court.

The arrest warrant must include the person's name or a sufficient physical description by which he or she can be identified and all details known to the officer that would lead a reasonable person to believe the suspect committed the crime (Legal Information Institute, n.d.a). Arrest warrants do not expire. They remain valid until the suspect is arrested (warrant, n.d.).

Officers must be familiar with the Fourth Amendment, state statute, and department policy concerning the procurement and service of an arrest warrant. Arrest warrants are a vital piece of the investigative function. Figures 4.1 and 4.2 provide an example of an arrest warrant and affidavit.

Arrest Report or Booking Report

Officers are often required to write a booking report when an arrestee is transported or delivered to a jail. Arrest report forms are typically just a single page in length and must be completed before an arrestee is transferred to the custody of the jail. The majority of the form consists of blanks for entering information or simple check boxes. Officers should not leave any section of the arrest report blank to ensure that information is not altered.

Figure 4.1   Sample Affidavit for an Arrest Warrant

This form is an example of an affidavit for an arrest warrant. The form may vary slightly in various jurisdictions. The affidavit is used to ask a judge to sign the arrest warrant.

AFFIDAVIT FOR PROBABLE CAUSE FOR ARREST WARRANT (Under Chapter 45, C.C.P.)

CAUSE NUMBER:_____

STATE OF TEXAS	§	**IN THE MUNICIPAL COURT**
VS.	§	**CITY OF** _____
_____	§	_____ **COUNTY, TEXAS**

AFFIDAVIT

My name is _____ and I have good reason to believe and do believe that the offense of: _____has been committed within the territorial limits of the City of _____, _____County, State of Texas, as set forth in the attached reports and documents that are incorporated herein as if set forth in their entirety.

Affiant's belief is based on the following:

☐   Affiant's personal investigation of this offense, which is described in the attached reports and documents.

☐   Information received from _____, a peace officer who Affiant believes to be credible and who personally participated in the investigation of this offense, whose information is described in the attached reports and documents.

_____
Affiant

BEFORE ME, the undersigned authority, on this day personally appeared _____, known to me to be the person whose name is subscribed to the above statement, and after being sworn by me, duly stated that the statements contained herein are true and correct to the best of his/her knowledge.

Sworn to and subscribed before me on this the _____ day of_____, 20___.

_____
(Judge)(Clerk)(Notary Public in and for the State of Texas)

Source: Warrants and Capias Forms book, 2011, http://www.tmcec.com/public/files/File/Resources/Final%20 Website%20Forms%20Book/PDF/04-Warrants%20&%20Capias.pdf.

Figure 4.2 Sample Arrest Warrant

This form is a sample arrest warrant. The format of the form may appear slightly different depending on the jurisdiction. The arrest warrant is the judge's order to arrest a person and bring them before the court.

WARRANT OF ARREST: JUDGE (Art. 45.014, C.C.P.)

CAUSE NUMBER:_____

STATE OF TEXAS	§	**IN THE MUNICIPAL COURT**
VS.	§	**CITY OF** _____
_____	§	_____ **COUNTY, TEXAS**

THE STATE OF TEXAS, TO ANY PEACE OFFICER OF THE STATE OF TEXAS - GREETINGS:

You are hereby commanded to arrest _____ , Defendant, and bring (him) (her) before the Municipal Court named above on the _____ day of _____ , 20___. Said Defendant has been accused of the fine-only misdemeanor offense: _____
_____ ,
which is against the laws of the State of Texas and/or against the city ordinances of said city.

Herein fail not, but make due service and return of this warrant of arrest, showing how you executed the same.

Signed this _____ day of _____ , 20__.

(municipal court seal)

_____
Judge, Municipal Court

City of _____

_____ County, Texas

....

OFFICER'S RETURN

Came to hand the _____ day of _____ , 20__, at _____ o'clock ___.m. and executed on the _____ day of_____ , 20__, at _____ o'clock ___.m. by _____
_____.

_____
Peace Officer

> **Editor's Note:** Judges in counties with population of more than two million and without a county attorney may not issue a warrant for issuance of a bad check unless the district attorney has approved the complaint or affidavit on which the warrant is based.

Source: Warrants and Capias Forms book, 2011, http://www.tmcec.com/public/files/File/Resources/Final%20Website%20Forms%20Book/PDF/04-Warrants%20&%20Capias.pdf.

Any section of the form not utilized should be marked through completely and initialed by the officer.

Many agencies require the arresting officer complete a detailed incident report in addition to an arrest report. In this case, the complete details of the incident are included in the initial incident report. The narrative section of the arrest report (as noted in Example 4.1) can be just one or two paragraphs in length since it requires only the details that establish probable cause for the arrest.

Some agencies do not require the arresting officer to complete an incident report form for all arrests. The arrest report in this case must, then, include all the details of the incident just as would be required for an incident report. Finally, if an individual is arrested for an outstanding warrant, some agencies do not require the details of the initial incident and probable cause for the arrest to be included in the arrest report. These details are required to be presented to a judge in the form of an affidavit for an arrest warrant. If the judge finds probable cause exists for the arrest of an individual, only then is the arrest warrant issued. In these cases, it is often sufficient for the narrative to simply state "The subject was arrested on a confirmed warrants hit." Figure 4.3 is an example of an arrest warrant.

Traffic Crash Reports

According to a Florida Department of Motor Vehicles report, there were almost 400,000 traffic crashes in the state in 2016, and that number is rising each year (Florida Department of Highway Safety and Motor Vehicles, n.d.). That same year, 34,439 people were killed nationally in fatal crashes (National Highway Traffic Safety Administration, n.d.). Some sheriff's offices do not investigate traffic crashes, so the job of writing traffic crash reports falls primarily upon officers with state highway patrol agencies and municipal police departments.

Officers collect and record a large amount of data during a traffic crash investigation. Much of this data is collected through the use of simple check and fill-in boxes. Commonly collected traffic crash data include details of the crash location, driver and passenger information, road and weather conditions, vehicles, pedestrians, or bicycles involved in the crash, violations, and suspected alcohol or drug involvement. Traffic crash reports also include space for a narrative and a diagram of the crash event.

These data are used in various ways both within and outside of the police agency. The analysis of traffic crash data is used by police in making decisions for traffic enforcement, by highway safety offices to evaluate highway safety programs, by engineers in road construction, by researchers to identify crash patterns, and by legislators to implement programs and draft data-driven legislation (National Highway Traffic Safety Administration, 2017).

Laws governing traffic crash reporting requirements are different in each state. All states require a traffic crash investigation and report by an officer in cases of death or injury. But in crashes without injuries that do not exceed a damage threshold—typically between $300 and $1,000 depending on the state—crash victims may complete a self-report (shown in Figure 4.4) or short form without the assistance of an officer. In Florida, for example, a

(Text continues on p. 77.)

Figure 4.3 Sample Arrest Report

This form represents a standardized arrest report used by many agencies. The format of the form may differ across jurisdictions. A unique feature of this form is the release block. Rather than requiring a separate release form, this format captures all data related to the arrest in a single form.

ALABAMA UNIFORM ARREST REPORT

DOMESTIC VIOLENCE DUAL ARREST ☐

Fingerprinted: ① Yes ② No
R84 Completed: ① Yes ② No

OFFICER'S WORK PRODUCT MAY NOT BE PUBLIC INFORMATION

IDENTIFICATION

1 ORI # A L | 2 Agency Name | 3 Case # | 4 SFX

5 Last, First, Middle Name | 6 Alias AKA

7 Sex ① M ② F | 8 Race ① W ② B ③ A ④ I | 9 Ethnicity ① Hispanic ② Other ____ | 10 Hgt | 11 Wgt | 12 Eye | 13 Hair | 14 Skin | 15 ① Scars ② Marks ③ Tattoos ④ Amputations

16 Place of Birth (City, County State) | 17 SSN | 18 Date of Birth M D Y | 19 Age | 20 Miscellaneous ID #

21 SID # | 22 Fingerprint Class — Key Major Primary SCDV Sub-Secondary Final / Henry Class / NCIC Class | 23 DL# | 24 St

25 FBI # | 26 Identification Comments

27 ① Resident ② Non-Resident | 28 Home Address (Street, City, State, Zip) | 29 Residence Phone ( ) | 30 Occupation (Be Specific)

31 Employer (Name of Company/School) | 32 Business Address (Street, City, State, Zip) | 33 Business Phone ( )

ARREST

34 Location of Arrest (Street, City, State, Zip) | 35 Sector # | 36 Arrested for Your Jurisdiction? ① In State ② Out of State Agency ☐ Yes ☐ No

37 Condition of Arrestee: ① Drunk ② Drinking ③ Sober ④ Drugs | 38 Resist Arrest? ① Yes ② No | 39 Injuries? ① None ② Officer ③ Arrestee | 40 Armed? ① Y ② N | 41 Description of Weapon ① Handgun ② Rifle ③ Shotgun ④ Other Firearm ⑤ Other Weapon

42 Date of Arrest M D Y | 43 Time of Arrest : ☐ AM ☐ PM ☐ MIL | 44 Day of Arrest S M T W T F S / 1 2 3 4 5 6 7 | 45 Type of Arrest? ① On View ② Call ③ Warrant | 46 Arrested Before? ① Yes ② No ③ Unknown

47 Charge - 1 ① Fel ② Misd | 48 UCR Code | 49 Charge - 2 ① Fel ② Misd | 50 UCR Code

51 State Code/Local Ordinance | 52 Warrant # | 53 Date Issued M D Y | 54 State Code/Local Ordinance | 55 Warrant # | 56 Date Issued M D Y

57 Charge - 3 ① Fel ② Misd | 58 UCR Code | 59 Charge - 4 ① Fel ② Misd | 60 UCR Code

61 State Code/Local Ordinance | 62 Warrant # | 63 Date Issued M D Y | 64 State Code/Local Ordinance | 65 Warrant # | 66 Date Issued M D Y

67 Arrest Disposition ① Held ② Bail ③ Released ④ Tot - LE ⑤ Other | 68 If Out On Release What Type? | 69 Arrested with (1) Accomplice (Full Name) / 70 Arrested with (2) Accomplice (Full Name)

VEHICLE

71 VYR | 72 VMA | 73 VMO | 74 VST | 75 VCO Top Bottom | 76 Tag # | 77 LIS | 78 LIY

79 VIN | 80 Impounded? ① Yes ② No | 81 Storage Location/Impound #

82 Other Evidence Seized/Property Seized | ☐ Continued in Narrative

JUVENILE

83 Juvenile Disposition: ① Handled and Released ② Ref. to Juvenile Court ③ Ref. to Welfare Agency ④ Ref. to Other Police Agency ⑤ Ref. to Adult Court | 84 Released To

85 Parent or Guardian (Last, First, Middle Name) | 86 Address (Street, City, State, Zip) | 87 Phone ( )

88 Parents Employer | 89 Occupation | 90 Address (Street, City, State, Zip) | 91 Phone ( )

RELEASE

92 Date and Time of Release M D Y : ① AM ② PM ③ MIL | 93 Releasing Officer Name | 94 Agency/Division | 95 ID #

96 Released To | 97 Agency/Division | 98 Agency Address

99 Personal Property Released to Arrestee ① Yes ② No ③ Partial | 100 Property Not Released/Held At: | 101 Property #

102 Remarks (Note Any Injuries at Time of Release)

Local Use

103 Signature of Receiving Officer | 104 Signature of Releasing Officer | State Use

MULTIPLE CASES CLOSED: 105 Case # | 106 SFX | 107 Case # | 108 SFX | 109 Case # | 110 SFX | 111 MULTIPLE CASES CLOSED NARRATIVE ☐ Y ☐ N

112 Arresting Officer (Last, First, M.) | 113 ID # | 114 Arresting Officer (Last, First, M.) | 115 ID # | 116 Supervisor ID # | 117 Watch Cmdr. ID #

TYPE OR PRINT IN BLACK INK ONLY

ACJIC - 11-06

Figure 4.4 Florida Self-Report Traffic Crash Form

This form is an example of a report used by those involved in a traffic crash, which meets certain requirements, to self-report the crash without the assistance of an officer. Many jurisdictions authorize the use of this type of form for drivers to report minor crashes that do not involve injuries.

	HSMV Report Number
	FOR AGENCY USE ONLY

☐ Driver Report of Traffic Crash (Self Report)
☐ Driver Exchange of Information

REPORTING AGENCY CASE NUMBER	DATE OF CRASH	TIME OF CRASH	AM ☐ PM ☐
FOR AGENCY USE ONLY			

COUNTY OF CRASH (County Code)	PLACE OR CITY OF CRASH (City Code)	Check if Within City Limits ☐	CRASH OCCURRED ON STREET, ROAD, HIGHWAY

AT STREET ADDRESS #   OR   FEET   MILES   N S E W ☐☐☐☐   AT / FROM INTERSECTION WITH STREET, ROAD, HIGHWAY   OR FROM MILEPOST#

SECTION ONE ☐ VEHICLE   ☐ NON-MOTORIST   (optional) EMAIL OWNER/DRIVER

YEAR	MAKE (Chevy, Ford, Etc.)	VEHICLE BODY TYPE (Car, Truck, Etc.)	VEHICLE LICENSE NUMBER	STATE	VIN

INSURANCE COMPANY	INSURANCE POLICY NUMBER

NAME OF VEHICLE OWNER	(Check if same as Driver) ☐	CURRENT ADDRESS (Number and Street)	CITY AND STATE	ZIP CODE

NAME OF DRIVER (Take From Driver License)/NON-MOTORIST	CURRENT ADDRESS (Number and Street)	CITY AND STATE	ZIP CODE

DRIVER LICENSE NUMBER	STATE	DL TYPE	DRIVER/NON-MOTORIST HOME PHONE ( ) Area Code	DRIVER/NON-MOTORIST BUSINESS PHONE ( ) Area Code	SEX	DATE OF BIRTH

NAME OF PASSENGER	CURRENT ADDRESS (Number and Street)	CITY AND STATE	ZIP CODE

NAME OF PASSENGER	CURRENT ADDRESS (Number and Street)	CITY AND STATE	ZIP CODE

SECTION TWO ☐ VEHICLE   ☐ NON-MOTORIST   (optional) EMAIL OWNER/DRIVER

YEAR	MAKE (Chevy, Ford, Etc.)	VEHICLE BODY TYPE (Car, Truck, Etc.)	VEHICLE LICENSE NUMBER	STATE	VIN

INSURANCE COMPANY	INSURANCE POLICY NUMBER

NAME OF VEHICLE OWNER	(Check if same as Driver) ☐	CURRENT ADDRESS (Number and Street)	CITY AND STATE	ZIP CODE

NAME OF DRIVER (Take From Driver License)/NON-MOTORIST	CURRENT ADDRESS (Number and Street)	CITY AND STATE	ZIP CODE

DRIVER LICENSE NUMBER	STATE	DL TYPE	DRIVER/NON-MOTORIST HOME PHONE ( ) Area Code	DRIVER/NON-MOTORIST BUSINESS PHONE ( ) Area Code	SEX	DATE OF BIRTH

NAME OF PASSENGER	CURRENT ADDRESS (Number and Street)	CITY AND STATE	ZIP CODE

NAME OF PASSENGER	CURRENT ADDRESS (Number and Street)	CITY AND STATE	ZIP CODE

SECTION THREE ☐ VEHICLE   ☐ NON-MOTORIST   (optional) EMAIL OWNER/DRIVER

YEAR	MAKE (Chevy, Ford, Etc.)	VEHICLE BODY TYPE (Car, Truck, Etc.)	VEHICLE LICENSE NUMBER	STATE	VIN

INSURANCE COMPANY	INSURANCE POLICY NUMBER

NAME OF VEHICLE OWNER	(Check if same as Driver) ☐	CURRENT ADDRESS (Number and Street)	CITY AND STATE	ZIP CODE

NAME OF DRIVER (Take From Driver License)/NON-MOTORIST	CURRENT ADDRESS (Number and Street)	CITY AND STATE	ZIP CODE

DRIVER LICENSE NUMBER	STATE	DL TYPE	DRIVER/NON-MOTORIST HOME PHONE ( ) Area Code	DRIVER/NON-MOTORIST BUSINESS PHONE ( ) Area Code	SEX	DATE OF BIRTH

NAME OF PASSENGER	CURRENT ADDRESS (Number and Street)	CITY AND STATE	ZIP CODE

NAME OF PASSENGER	CURRENT ADDRESS (Number and Street)	CITY AND STATE	ZIP CODE

WITNESSES

(1) NAME	CURRENT ADDRESS	CITY AND STATE	ZIP CODE	(2) NAME	CURRENT ADDRESS	CITY AND STATE	ZIP CODE

SIGNATURE OF DRIVER MAKING REPORT   DATE

YOU MUST READ AND COMPLY WITH THE INSTRUCTIONS ON THE BACK OF THIS FORM

HSMV 90011S (rev 06/2012)

IF YOU WERE TOLD TO COMPLETE AND FORWARD THIS REPORT TO THE DEPARTMENT, PLEASE REFER TO THE FOLLOWING INSTRUCTIONS AND EXAMPLE:

			HSMV Report Number		

[X] Driver Report of Traffic Crash (Self Report)	REPORTING AGENCY CASE NUMBER	DATE OF CRASH 01-01-10	TIME OF CRASH 11:30	AM [X]	PM
[ ] Driver Exchange of Information					

COUNTY OF CRASH (County Code) PINELLAS (04)	PLACE OR CITY OF CRASH (City Code) ST. PETERSBURG (64)	Check if Within City Limits [ ]	CRASH OCCURRED ON STREET, ROAD, HIGHWAY 2ⁿᵈ STREET SOUTH
AT STREET ADDRESS # OR FEET MILES 0	N [ ] S [ ] E [ ] W [ ]	AT / FROM INTERSECTION WITH STREET, ROAD, HIGHWAY U.S. 19	OR FROM MILEPOST#

SECTION ONE [X] VEHICLE [ ] NON-MOTORIST (optional) EMAIL OWNER/DRIVER

YEAR 80	MAKE (Chevy, Ford, Etc.) FORD	VEHICLE BODY TYPE (Car, Truck, Etc) CAR	VEHICLE LICENSE NUMBER ABC-123	STATE FL	VIN

INSURANCE COMPANY INSURANCE COMPANY OF FL	INSURANCE POLICY NUMBER I.C.F. 120000

NAME OF VEHICLE OWNER JOHN DOE	(Check if same as Driver) [ ]	CURRENT ADDRESS (Number and Street) 1111 FIRST STREET NORTH	CITY AND STATE PETERSBURG, FL	ZIP CODE 33731

NAME OF DRIVER (Take From Driver License)/NON-MOTORIST BILL DOE	CURRENT ADDRESS (Number and Street) SAME AS OWNER	CITY AND STATE	ZIP CODE

DRIVER LICENSE NUMBER D 561345706000	STATE FL	DL TYPE	DRIVER/NON-MOTORIST HOME PHONE ( ) Area Code	DRIVER/NON-MOTORIST BUSINESS PHONE ( ) Area Code	SEX M	DATE OF BIRTH 01-01-70

NAME OF PASSENGER SALLEY DOE	CURRENT ADDRESS (Number and Street) SAME AS OWNER	CITY AND STATE	ZIP CODE
NAME OF PASSENGER	CURRENT ADDRESS (Number and Street)	CITY AND STATE	ZIP CODE

Effective July 1, 2012, Section 316.066(1)(e), Florida Statute, requires that "The driver of a vehicle that was in any manner involved in a crash resulting in damage to a vehicle or other property which does not require a law enforcement report shall, within 10 days after the crash, submit a written report of the crash to the department. The report shall be submitted on a form approved by the department."

- Keep a copy of this report for your records and for insurance purposes.
- Sign the report at the bottom of the front page.
- Mail this report to: **Florida Department of Highway Safety & Motor Vehicles**
  Crash Records
  2900 Apalachee Pkwy, MS 28
  Tallahassee, Florida 32399

Please use this space for comments and for listing any witnesses and/or additional passengers, stating which vehicle the passenger was in. For additional vehicles or other involved parties, please add additional front pages for this Driver Report of Traffic Crash.

Customers may send a copy of the form to an email address of their choosing. | **Email Copy of Form**

Once complete, submit this form via email to FLHSMV Traffic Crash Records. | **Click here to Submit**

Source: https://www.flhsmv.gov/ddl/ecrash/HSMV90011S.pdf.

Figure 4.5 Florida Traffic Crash Report

This is an example of a traffic crash form that would be completed by an officer. Notice the increased level of detail required to complete this form compared to the self-report form (Figure 4.4).

FLORIDA TRAFFIC CRASH REPORT

LONG FORM ☐   SHORT FORM ☐   UPDATE ☐

TOTAL # OF VEHICLE SECTION(S) _____

MAIL TO: DEPARTMENT OF HIGHWAY SAFETY & MOTOR VEHICLES
TRAFFIC CRASH RECORDS, NEIL KIRKMAN BUILDING
TALLAHASSEE, FL 32399-0537

TOTAL # OF PERSON SECTION(S) _____

TOTAL # OF NARRATIVE SECTION(S) _____

CRASH DATE	TIME OF CRASH	DATE OF REPORT	REPORTING AGENCY CASE NUMBER	HSMV CRASH REPORT NUMBER

CRASH IDENTIFIERS

COUNTY CODE	CITY CODE	COUNTY OF CRASH	PLACE OR CITY OF CRASH	CHECK IF WITHIN CITY LIMITS	TIME REPORTED	TIME DISPATCHED

TIME ON SCENE	TIME CLEARED SCENE	CHECK IF COMPLETED	REASON (If Investigation NOT Complete)	Notified By: 1 Motorist 2 Law Enforcement

ROADWAY INFORMATION (CHOOSE ONLY 1 OF 4 OPTIONS)

CRASH OCCURRED ON STREET, ROAD, HIGHWAY   ①   AT STREET ADDRESS #   ②   AT LATITUDE   AND   LONGITUDE

FEET   MILES   N S E W   ③   AT / FROM INTERSECTION WITH STREET, ROAD, HIGHWAY   OR FROM MILEPOST #   ④

Road System Identifier
1 Interstate
2 U.S.
3 State
4 County
5 Local
6 Turnpike/Toll
7 Forest Road
8 Private Roadway
9 Parking Lot
77 Other, Explain in Narrative

Type of Shoulder
1 Paved
2 Unpaved
3 Curb

Type of Intersection
1 Not at Intersection
2 Four-Way Intersection
3 T-Intersection
4 Y-Intersection
5 Traffic Circle
6 Roundabout
7 Five-Point, or More
77 Other, Explain in Narrative

CRASH INFORMATION (CHECK IF PICTURES TAKEN)

Light Condition
1 Daylight
2 Dusk
3 Dawn
4 Dark-Lighted
5 Dark-Not Lighted
6 Dark-Unknown Lighting
77 Other, Explain in Narrative
88 Unknown

Weather Condition
4 Fog, Smog, Smoke
5 Sleet/Hail/ Freezing Rain
6 Blowing Sand, Soil, Dirt
7 Severe Crosswinds
77 Other, Explain in Narrative
1 Clear
2 Cloudy
3 Rain

Roadway Surface Condition
5 Oil
6 Mud, Dirt, Gravel
7 Sand
8 Water (standing/moving)
77 Other, Explain in Narrative
88 Unknown
1 Dry
2 Wet
4 Ice/Frost

School Bus Related
1 No
2 Yes, School Bus Directly Involved
3 Yes, School Bus Indirectly Involved

Manner of Collision/Impact
4 Sideswipe, Same Direction
5 Sideswipe, Opposite Direction
6 Rear to Side
7 Rear to Rear
77 Other, Explain in Narrative
88 Unknown
1 Front to Rear
2 Front to Front
3 Angle

First Harmful Event

First Harmful Event within Interchange
1 No
2 Yes
88 Unknown

Non-Collision
1 Overturn/Rollover
2 Fire/Explosion
3 Immersion
4 Jackknife
5 Cargo/Equipment Loss or Shift
6 Fell/Jumped From Motor Vehicle
7 Thrown or Falling Object
8 Ran into Water/Canal
9 Other Non-Collision

Collision Non-Fixed Object
10 Pedestrian
11 Pedalcycle
12 Railway Vehicle (train, engine)
13 Animal
14 Motor Vehicle in Transport
15 Parked Motor Vehicle
16 Work Zone/Maintenance Equipment
17 Struck By Falling, Shifting Cargo
18 Other Non-Fixed Object

Collision with Fixed Object
19 Impact Attenuator/Crash Cushion
20 Bridge Overhead Structure
21 Bridge Pier or Support
22 Bridge Rail
23 Culvert
24 Curb
25 Ditch
26 Embankment
27 Guardrail Face
28 Guardrail End
29 Cable Barrier
30 Concrete Traffic Barrier
31 Other Traffic Barrier
32 Tree (standing)
33 Utility Pole/Light Support
34 Traffic Sign Support
35 Traffic Signal Support
36 Other Post, Pole or Support
37 Fence
38 Mailbox
39 Other Fixed Object (wall, building, tunnel, etc.)

First Harmful Event Location
1 On Roadway
2 Off Roadway
3 Shoulder
4 Median
6 Gore
7 Separator
8 In Parking Lane or Zone
9 Outside Right-of-way
10 Roadside
88 Unknown

First Harmful Event Relation to Junction
1 Non-Junction
2 Intersection
3 Intersection-Related
4 Driveway/Alley Access Related
5 Railway Grade Crossing
14 Entrance/Exit Ramp
15 Crossover - Related
16 Shared-Use Path or Trail
17 Acceleration/Deceleration Lane
18 Through Roadway
77 Other, Explain in Narrative
88 Unknown

Contributing Circumstances: Road
1 None
4 Work Zone (construction/ maintenance/utility)
6 Shoulders (none, low, soft, high)
7 Rut, Holes, Bumps
9 Worn, Travel-Polished Surface
10 Road Surface Condition (wet, icy, snow, slush, etc.)
11 Obstruction in Roadway
12 Debris
13 Traffic Control Device Inoperative, Missing or Obscured
14 Non-Highway Work
77 Other, Explain in Narrative
88 Unknown

Contributing Circumstances: Environment
1 None
2 Weather Conditions
3 Physical Obstruction(s)
4 Glare
5 Animal(s) in Roadway
77 Other, Explain in Narrative

Work Zone Related
1 No
2 Yes
88 Unknown

Crash in Work Zone
1 Before the First Work Zone Warning Sign
2 Advance Warning Area
3 Transition Area
4 Activity Area
5 Termination Area

Type of Work Zone
1 Lane Closure
2 Lane Shift/Crossover
3 Work on Shoulder or Median
4 Intermittent or Moving Work
77 Other, Explain in Narrative

Workers in Work Zone
1 No
2 Yes
88 Unknown

Law Enforcement in Work Zone
1 No
2 Officer Present
3 Law Enforcement Vehicle Only Present

WITNESSES

NAME	ADDRESS	CITY & STATE	ZIP CODE
NAME	ADDRESS	CITY & STATE	ZIP CODE
NAME	ADDRESS	CITY & STATE	ZIP CODE

NON VEHICLE PROPERTY DAMAGE

VEHICLE #	PERSON #	PROPERTY DAMAGE – OTHER THAN VEHICLE	EST. AMOUNT	OWNER'S NAME ☐ (Check if Business)	ADDRESS	CITY & STATE	ZIP CODE
VEHICLE #	PERSON #	PROPERTY DAMAGE – OTHER THAN VEHICLE	EST. AMOUNT	OWNER'S NAME ☐ (Check if Business)	ADDRESS	CITY & STATE	ZIP CODE

HSMV 90010 S (E) (rev 06/13)

Page ___ of ___

VEHICLE #		Check if Commercial		REPORTING AGENCY CASE NUMBER	HSMV CRASH REPORT NUMBER

1 Vehicle in Transport
2 Parked Motor Vehicle
3 Working Vehicle

VEHICLE LICENSE NUMBER	STATE	REGISTRATION EXPIRES	Check if Permanent Registration	VIN

Hit and Run
1 No
2 Yes
88 Unknown

YEAR	MAKE	MODEL	STYLE	COLOR	DAMAGE: 1 Disabling 4 Minor 2 Functional 88 Unknown 3 None	EST. AMOUNT

INSURANCE COMPANY	INSURANCE POLICY NUMBER	Towed due to Damage: 1 No 2 Yes	VEHICLE REMOVED BY	1 Rotation 2 Owner Request 3 Driver 77 Other, Explain in Narrative

NAME OF VEHICLE OWNER (Check if Business)	CURRENT ADDRESS	CITY & STATE	ZIP CODE

TRAILER #	LICENSE NUMBER	STATE	REGISTRATION EXPIRES	Check if Permanent Registration	VIN	YEAR	MAKE	LENGTH	AXLES

TRAILER #	LICENSE NUMBER	STATE	REGISTRATION EXPIRES	Check if Permanent Registration	VIN	YEAR	MAKE	LENGTH	AXLES

VEHICLE TRAVELING   N   S   E   W   Off-Road   Unknown

ON STREET, ROAD, HIGHWAY	AT EST. SPEED	POSTED SPEED	TOTAL LANES

HAZ. MAT. RELEASED 1 No 2 Yes 88 Unknown	HAZ. MAT PLACARD 1 No 2 Yes 88 Unknown	HAZ. MAT. NUMBER	HAZ. MAT. CLASS	Area of Initial Impact		Most Damaged Area

18 Undercarriage 18
19 Overturn 19
20 Windshield 20
21 Trailer 21

MOTOR CARRIER NAME	US DOT NUMBER

MOTOR CARRIER ADDRESS	CITY & STATE	ZIP CODE	PHONE NUMBER

Vehicle Body Type

1 Passenger Car
2 Passenger Van
3 Pickup
7 Motor Home
8 Bus
11 Motorcycle
12 Moped
13 All Terrain Vehicle (ATV)
15 Low Speed Vehicle
16 (Sport) Utility Vehicle
17 Cargo Van (10,000 lbs (4,536 kg) or less)
18 Motor Coach
19 Other Light Trucks (10,000 lbs (4,536 kg) or less)
20 Medium/Heavy Trucks (more than 10,000 lbs (4,536 kg))
21 Farm Labor Vehicle
77 Other, Explain in Narrative
88 Unknown

Trafficway

1 Two-Way, Not Divided
2 Two-Way, Not Divided, with a Continuous Left Turn Lane
3 Two-Way, Divided, Unprotected (painted >4 feet) Median
4 Two-Way, Divided, Positive Median Barrier
5 One-Way Trafficway
88 Unknown

Commercial Motor Vehicle Configuration

1 Vehicle 10,000 lbs or less Placarded for Hazardous Materials
2 Single-Unit Truck (2-axle and GVWR more than 10,000 lbs (4,536 kg))
3 Single-Unit Truck (3 or more axles)
4 Truck Pulling Trailer(s)
5 Truck Tractor (bobtail)
6 Truck Tractor/Semi-Trailer
7 Truck Tractor/Double
8 Truck Tractor/Triple
9 Truck more than 10,000 lbs (4,536 kg), Cannot Classify
10 Bus/Large Van (seats for 9-15 occupants, including driver)
11 Bus (seats for more than 15 occupants, including driver)
77 Other, Explain in Narrative
88 Unknown

Comm/Non-Commercial

1 Interstate Carrier
2 Intrastate Carrier
3 Not in Commerce/Government
4 Not in Commerce/Other Truck

Trailer Type

TRAILER 1   TRAILER 2

1 Single Semi Trailer
2 Tandem Semi Trailer
3 Tank Trailer
4 Saddle Mount/Trailer
5 Boat Trailer
6 Utility Trailer
7 House Trailer
8 Pole Trailer
9 Towed Vehicle
10 Auto Transport
77 Other, Explain in Narrative
88 Unknown

Cargo Body Type

1 No Cargo
2 Bus

3 Van/Enclosed Box
4 Hopper
5 Pole-Trailer
6 Cargo Tank
7 Flatbed
8 Dump
9 Concrete Mixer
10 Auto Transport
11 Garbage/Refuse
12 Log
13 Intermodal Container Chassis
14 Vehicle Towing Another Vehicle
15 Not Applicable (vehicle 10,000 lbs (4,536kg) or less not displaying HM placard)
77 Other, Explain in Narrative
88 Unknown

Most Harmful Event

Sequence of Events

1st   2nd

3rd   4th

Roadway Grade

1 Level
2 Hillcrest
3 Uphill
4 Downhill
5 Sag (bottom)

Non-Collision

1 Overturn/Rollover
2 Fire/Explosion
3 Immersion
4 Jackknife
5 Cargo/Equipment Loss or Shift
6 Fell/Jumped From Motor Vehicle
7 Thrown or Falling Object
8 Ran Into Water/ Canal
9 Other Non-Collision

[40-46 Sequence of Events only]
40 Equipment Failure (blown tire, brake failure, etc.)
41 Separation of Units
42 Ran Off Roadway, Right
43 Ran Off Roadway, Left
44 Cross Median
45 Cross Centerline
46 Downhill Runaway

Comm GVWR/GCWR

1 10,000 lbs (4,536 kg) or less
2 10,001-26,000 lbs (4,536-11,793 kg)
3 More than 26,000 lbs (11,793 kg)
4 Not Applicable

Collision with Non-Fixed Object

10 Pedestrian
11 Pedalcycle
12 Railway Vehicle (train, engine)
13 Animal
14 Motor Vehicle in Transport
15 Parked Motor Vehicle
16 Work Zone/Maintenance Equipment
17 Struck By Falling, Shifting Cargo or Anything Set in Motion by Motor Vehicle
18 Other Non-Fixed Object

Collision Fixed Object

19 Impact Attenuator/Crash Cushion
20 Bridge Overhead Structure
21 Bridge Pier or Support
22 Bridge Rail
23 Culvert
24 Curb
25 Ditch
26 Embankment
27 Guardrail Face
28 Guardrail End
29 Cable Barrier
30 Concrete Traffic Barrier
31 Other Traffic Barrier
32 Tree (standing)
33 Utility Pole/Light Support
34 Traffic Sign Support
35 Traffic Signal Support
36 Other Post, Pole, or Support
37 Fence
38 Mailbox
39 Other Fixed Object (wall, building, tunnel, etc.)

Emergency Vehicle Use

1 No
2 Yes
88 Unknown

Roadway Alignment

1 Straight
2 Curve Right
3 Curve Left

Vehicle Maneuver Action

1 Straight Ahead
3 Turning Left
4 Backing
5 Turning Right
6 Changing Lanes
8 Parked
10 Making U-Turn
11 Overtaking/Passing
13 Stopped in Traffic
14 Slowing
15 Negotiating a Curve
16 Leaving Traffic Lane
17 Entering Traffic Lane
77 Other, Explain in Narrative
88 Unknown

Traffic Control Device For This Vehicle

1 No Controls
4 School Zone Sign/Device
5 Traffic Control Signal
6 Stop Sign
7 Yield Sign
8 Flashing Signal
9 Railway Crossing Device
10 Person (including Flagman, Officer, Guard, etc.)
13 Warning Sign
77 Other, Explain in Narrative
88 Unknown

Vehicle Defects

1 None
2 Brakes
3 Tires
4 Lights (head, signal, tail)
6 Steering
7 Wipers
9 Exhaust System
10 Body, Doors
11 Power Train
12 Suspension
13 Wheels
14 Windows/Windshield
15 Mirrors
16 Truck Coupling/Trailer Hitch/Safety Chains
77 Other, Explain in Narrative
88 Unknown

Special Function of Motor Vehicle

1 No Special Function
2 Farm Vehicle
3 Police
7 Taxi
8 Military
9 Ambulance
10 Fire Truck
11 Farm Labor Transport
12 School Bus
13 Transit/Commuter Bus
14 Intercity Bus
15 Charter/Tour Bus
16 Shuttle Bus
17 Farm Labor Bus
88 Unknown

VIOLATIONS

PERSON #	NAME OF VIOLATOR	FL STATUTE NUMBER	CHARGE	CITATION NUMBER
PERSON #	NAME OF VIOLATOR	FL STATUTE NUMBER	CHARGE	CITATION NUMBER
PERSON #	NAME OF VIOLATOR	FL STATUTE NUMBER	CHARGE	CITATION NUMBER

HSMV 90010 S (V/P) (rev 06/13)

Page ___ of ___

(Continued)

Figure 4.5 (Continued)

PERSON #

REPORTING AGENCY CASE NUMBER	HSMV CRASH REPORT NUMBER

1 Driver / 2 Non-Motorist / 3 Passenger	VEHICLE #	NAME	PHONE NUMBER	Check if Recommend Driver Re-exam

CURRENT ADDRESS (Number and Street)	CITY & STATE	ZIP CODE

DATE OF BIRTH	SEX: 1 Male 2 Female 88 Unknown	DRIVER LICENSE NUMBER	STATE	EXPIRES	INJURY SEVERITY (INJ) 1 None 2 Possible 3 Non-incapacitating 4 Incapacitating 5 Fatal (within 30 days) 6 Non-Traffic Fatality

DRIVER

DL Type
1 A 2 B 3 C
4 D/Chauffeur
5 E/Operator
6 E/Oper – Rest
7 None

Required Endorsements
1 Yes
2 No
3 No Req. Endorsement

Driver's Actions at Time of Crash

1st / 2nd / 3rd / 4th

1 No Contributing Action
2 Operated MV in Careless or Negligent Manner
3 Failed to Yield Right-of- Way
4 Improper Backing
6 Improper Turn
10 Followed too Closely
11 Ran Red Light
12 Drove too Fast for Conditions
13 Ran Stop Sign
15 Improper Passing
17 Exceeded Posted Speed
21 Wrong Side of Wrong Way
25 Failed to Keep in Proper Lane
26 Ran off Roadway
27 Disregarded other Traffic Sign
28 Disregarded Other Road Markings
29 Over-Correcting/Over-Steering
30 Swerved or Avoided : Due to Wind, Slippery Surface, MV, Object, Non-Motorist in Roadway, etc.
31 Operated MV in Erratic, Reckless or Aggressive Manner
77 Other Contributing Action

Condition At Time of Crash
1 Apparently Normal
2 Asleep or Fatigued
3 Ill (sick) or Fainted
6 Seizure, Epilepsy, Blackout
7 Physically Impaired
8 Emotional (depression, angry, disturbed, etc.)
9 Under the Influence of Medications/Drugs/Alcohol
77 Other, Explain in Narrative
88 Unknown

Driver Distracted By
1 Not Distracted
2 Electronic Communication Devices (cell phone, etc.)
3 Other Electronic Device (navigation device, DVD player)
4 Other Inside the Vehicle (explain in narrative)
5 External Distraction (outside the vehicle, explain in narrative)
6 Texting
7 Inattentive
88 Unknown

Driver Vision Obstructions
1 Vision Not Obscured
2 Inclement Weather
3 Parked/Stopped Vehicle
4 Trees/Crops/Bushes
5 Load on Vehicle
6 Building/Fixed Object
7 Signs/Billboards
8 Fog
9 Smoke
10 Glare
77 All Other, Explain in Narrative

DRIVER OR PASSENGER

Helmet Use (HU)
1 DOT-Compliant Motorcycle Helmet
2 Other Helmet
3 No Helmet

Eye Protection (EP)
1 Yes
2 No
3 Not Applicable

Restraint Systems (RS)
1 Not Applicable
2 None Used - Motor Vehicle Occupant
3 Shoulder and Lap Belt Used
4 Shoulder Belt Only Used
5 Lap Belt Only Used
6 Restraint Used - Type Unknown
7 Child Restraint System - Forward Facing
8 Child Restraint System - Rear Facing
9 Booster Seat
10 Child Restraint Type Unknown
77 Other, Explain in Narrative

DRIVER OR PASSENGER

Motor Vehicle Seating Position:

LOCATION: SEAT ROW OTHER (LOC)

Seat
1 Left
2 Middle
3 Right
77 Other (explain in narrative)
88 Unknown

Row
1 Front
2 Second
3 Third
4 Fourth
77 Other Row
88 Unknown

Other
1 Not Applicable
2 Sleeper Section of Truck Cab
3 Other Enclosed Cargo Area
4 Unenclosed Cargo Area
5 Trailing Unit
6 Riding on Motor Vehicle Exterior (non-trailing unit)
88 Unknown

Ejection (EJECT)
1 Not Ejected
2 Ejected, Totally
3 Ejected, Partially
4 Not Applicable
88 Unknown

Air Bag Deployed (ABD)
1 Not Applicable
2 Not Deployed
3 Deployed-Front
4 Deployed-Side
5 Deployed-Other (knee, air belt, etc.)
6 Deployed-Combination
7 Deployed-Curtain
88 Deployment Unknown

NON MOTORIST

Non-Motorist Description
1 Pedestrian
2 Other Pedestrian (wheelchair, person in a building, skater, pedestrian conveyance, etc.)
3 Bicyclist
4 Other Cyclist
5 Occupant of Motor Vehicle Not in Transport (parked, etc.)
6 Occupant of a Non-Motor Vehicle Transportation Device
7 Unknown Type of Non-Motorist

Non-Motorist Location At Time of Crash
1 Intersection - Marked Crosswalk
2 Intersection - Unmarked Crosswalk
3 Intersection – Other
4 Midblock - Marked Crosswalk
5 Travel Lane - Other Location
6 Bicycle Lane
7 Shoulder/Roadside
8 Sidewalk
9 Median/Crossing Island
10 Driveway Access
11 Shared-Use Path or Trail
12 Non-Trafficway Area
77 Other, Explain in Narrative
88 Unknown

Action Prior to Crash

1 Crossing Roadway
2 Waiting to Cross Roadway
3 Walking/Cycling Along Roadway with Traffic (in or adjacent to travel lane)
4 Walking/Cycling Along Roadway Against Traffic (in or adjacent to travel lane)
5 Walking/Cycling on Sidewalk
6 In Roadway -- Other (working, playing, etc.)
7 Adjacent to Roadway (e.g., shoulder, median)
8 Going to or from School (K-12)
9 Working in Trafficway (incident response)
10 None
77 Other, Explain in Narrative
88 Unknown

Non-Motorist Actions/Circumstances

1st / 2nd

1 No Improper Action
2 Dart/Dash
3 Failure to Yield Right-of-Way
4 Failure to Obey Traffic Signs, Signals, or Officer
5 In Roadway Improperly (standing, lying, working, playing)
6 Disabled Vehicle Related (working on, pushing, leaving/approaching)
7 Entering/Exiting Parked/Standing Vehicle
8 Inattentive (talking, eating, etc)
9 Not Visible (dark clothing, no lighting, etc.)
10 Improper Turn/Merge
11 Improper Passing
12 Wrong-Way Riding or Walking
77 Other, Explain in Narrative
88 Unknown

Safety Equipment
1 None
2 Helmet
3 Protective Pads Used (elbows, knees, shins, etc.)
4 Reflective Clothing (jacket, backpack, etc.)
5 Lighting
6 Not Applicable
77 Other, Explain in Narrative
88 Unknown

ALCOHOL/DRUG/EMS

SUSPECTED ALCOHOL USE: 1 No 2 Yes 88 Unknown	ALCOHOL TESTED: 1 Test Not Given 2 Test Refused 3 Test Given 88 Unknown, if Tested	ALCOHOL TEST TYPE: 1 Blood 2 Breath 3 Urine 77 Other, Explain in Narrative	ALCOHOL TEST RESULT: 1 Pending 2 Completed 88 Unknown	BAC	SUSPECTED DRUG USE: 1 No 2 Yes 88 Unknown	DRUG TESTED: 1 Test Not Given 2 Test Refused 3 Test Given 88 Unknown, if Tested	DRUG TEST TYPE: 1 Blood 3 Urine 77 Other, Explain in Narrative	DRUG TEST RESULT: 1 Positive 2 Negative 3 Pending 88 Unknown

SOURCE OF TRANSPORT TO MEDICAL FACILITY 1 Not Transported 2 EMS 3 Law Enforcement 77 Other, Explain in Narrative 88 Unknown	EMS AGENCY NAME OR ID	EMS RUN NUMBER	MEDICAL FACILITY TRANSPORTED TO

ADDITIONAL PASSENGERS

PERSON #	VEHICLE #	NAME	DATE OF BIRTH	INJ	SEX	LOC: S	R	O	EJECT	HU	EP	ABD	RS

CURRENT ADDRESS (Number and Street)	CITY & STATE	ZIP CODE

SOURCE OF TRANSPORT TO MEDICAL FACILITY 1 Not Transported 2 EMS 3 Law Enforcement 77 Other, Explain in Narrative 88 Unknown	EMS AGENCY NAME OR ID	EMS RUN NUMBER	MEDICAL FACILITY TRANSPORTED TO

PERSON #	VEHICLE #	NAME	DATE OF BIRTH	INJ	SEX	LOC: S	R	O	EJECT	HU	EP	ABD	RS

CURRENT ADDRESS (Number and Street)	CITY & STATE	ZIP CODE

SOURCE OF TRANSPORT TO MEDICAL FACILITY 1 Not Transported 2 EMS 3 Law Enforcement 77 Other, Explain in Narrative 88 Unknown	EMS AGENCY NAME OR ID	EMS RUN NUMBER	MEDICAL FACILITY TRANSPORTED TO

HSMV 90010 S (V/P) (rev 06/13)

Page ___ of ___

NARRATIVE	REPORTING AGENCY CASE NUMBER	HSMV CRASH REPORT NUMBER

ADDITIONAL PASSENGERS

PERSON #	VEHICLE #	NAME	DATE OF BIRTH	INJ	SEX	LOC: S	R	O	EJECT	HU	EP	ABD	RS
		CURRENT ADDRESS (Number and Street)	CITY & STATE			ZIP CODE							

SOURCE OF TRANSPORT TO MEDICAL FACILITY 1 Not Transported 2 EMS 3 Law Enforcement 77 Other, Explain in Narrative 88 Unknown	EMS AGENCY NAME OR ID	EMS RUN NUMBER	MEDICAL FACILITY TRANSPORTED TO

PERSON #	VEHICLE #	NAME	DATE OF BIRTH	INJ	SEX	LOC: S	R	O	EJECT	HU	EP	ABD	RS
		CURRENT ADDRESS (Number and Street)	CITY & STATE			ZIP CODE							

SOURCE OF TRANSPORT TO MEDICAL FACILITY 1 Not Transported 2 EMS 3 Law Enforcement 77 Other, Explain in Narrative 88 Unknown	EMS AGENCY NAME OR ID	EMS RUN NUMBER	MEDICAL FACILITY TRANSPORTED TO

ADDITIONAL VIOLATIONS

PERSON #	NAME OF VIOLATOR	FL STATUTE NUMBER	CHARGE	CITATION NUMBER
PERSON #	NAME OF VIOLATOR	FL STATUTE NUMBER	CHARGE	CITATION NUMBER

REPORTING OFFICER

ID/BADGE NUMBER	RANK & NAME	DEPARTMENT	FHP	SO	PD	OTHER

HSMV 90010 S (N/D) (rev 06/13)

Page ___ of ___

Figure 4.5 (Continued)

DIAGRAM	REPORTING AGENCY CASE NUMBER	HSMV CRASH REPORT NUMBER

HSMV 90010 S (N/D) (rev 06/13)   Page ___ of ___

(Text continued from p. 68.)

driver can complete a self-report or traffic crash form online without the need of an officer at the crash scene. Although the formats of traffic crash reporting forms vary widely among jurisdictions, all traffic crash reports require that detailed information be collected and recorded.

CHAPTER SUMMARY

Police officers and investigators are often faced with complex cases. These cases often necessitate a variety of forms in addition to a basic incident report form. This chapter discusses the supplemental report, the arrest report, the evidence form, the arrest warrant, and the traffic crash report. Each of these reports requires that officers write a narrative.

Each supplemental form has a specific use. The supplemental report is used to add additional information to the incident report. The arrest report is used to document the probable cause for a defendant's arrest. The evidence form is used to identify items seized by an officer. An arrest warrant is used when probable cause has been obtained for a defendant's arrest. And the traffic crash report is used to list the persons, vehicles, and circumstances surrounding a traffic crash.

QUESTIONS FOR CONSIDERATION

1. Which constitutional amendment must be considered when obtaining a sworn statement from a suspect?

2. List the circumstances when a supplemental report form would be used.

3. Describe a classmate's watch or a piece of jewelry using the technique described in the Evidence Report section of this chapter.

4. Using the sample arrest report (Figure 4.3), interview a classmate and complete the Identification section.

5. Using the traffic crash form provided in Figure 4.4, complete Section One using your identification and vehicle information.

Search Warrants, Affidavits, and Sworn Statements

Anyone who has watched the news for more than a few hours has heard reports of police officers searching individuals' homes. In recent high profile cases in the United States, the media has reported police searches in the homes of Nikolas Cruz, accused of killing 17 people in a Florida school shooting; Devon Patrick Kelley, who killed 26 people in a Texas church; and Todd Kohlhepp, a registered sex offender who pleaded guilty in South Carolina to seven counts of murder, two counts of kidnapping, and one count of criminal sexual assault (Lohr, 2017). In each of these cases and in many others like them, the police searched the homes of the suspects to secure any evidence leading to their convictions and/or to explain why the crimes may have occurred.

Additionally, the police rely on statements made by suspects, victims, and witnesses in criminal investigations. When law enforcement officers interview suspects, victims, and witnesses regarding criminal activity, they ask the individuals to write their statements on paper. These are considered written sworn statements and can be used as evidence in court.

This chapter discusses search warrants, affidavits, and sworn statements. Students are provided examples of each of these forms as well.

What Is a Search Warrant?

A search warrant is a writ issued upon probable cause authorizing a specific action. Search warrants are signed by authorized court personnel—usually judges or magistrates—allowing the police to search a specific place without the owner's or occupant's consent (Legal Information Institute, n.d.b). The police use search warrants to find property or other criminal evidence to bring before the court in criminal cases. Search warrants are required under the Fourth Amendment of the United States Constitution for the police to conduct a search, with very few exceptions.

The Fourth Amendment and Limits to Searches

As discussed in Chapter 6, the Fourth Amendment applies to arrest warrants. The Fourth Amendment also applies to search warrants by providing protection to individuals from unreasonable searches and seizures by the government. Under this amendment, individuals have the right to be secure from the government in their home and with their property. Of important note in the Fourth Amendment is the key word— *unreasonable*. Because there is a multitude of interpretations of what *unreasonable* means, the U.S. Supreme Court has reviewed many cases on the Fourth Amendment. For the most part, the U.S. Supreme Court has determined these cases according to two interests: (1) Is the search unreasonable and a violation of the person's Fourth Amendment rights, and (2) is there a legitimate government interest as a basis for the search or seizure, such as public safety (United States Courts, n.d.). "The extent to which an individual is protected by the Fourth Amendment depends, in part, on the location of the search or seizure" (*Minnesota v. Carter*, 525 U.S. 83 (1998)).

The U.S. Supreme Court has determined that searches conducted without search warrants in individual homes are generally unreasonable (*Payton v. New York*, 445 U.S. 573 (1980)). However, there are some exceptions to this interpretation, such as when an individual provides consent to search his or her home (*Davis v. United States*, 328 U.S. 582 (1946)), if the search is incident to a lawful arrest (*United States v. Robinson*, 414 U.S. 218 (1973)), if there is probable cause to search and exigent circumstances (*Payton v. New York*, 445 U.S. 573 (1980)), and if the items are in plain view (*Maryland v. Macon*, 472 U.S. 463 (1985)). Even with these exceptions, a general rule for law enforcement is to secure a search warrant to search individual homes.

Law enforcement can also search people, schools, and cars. Each of these have their own standards under the U.S. Supreme Court's interpretations of the Fourth Amendment, but in general, if a police officer observes unusual conduct that could indicate criminal activity is occurring, the police officer can stop the suspicious person and make inquiries designed to confirm or dispel the officer's suspicions (*Terry v. Ohio*, 392 U.S. 1 (1968); *Minnesota v. Dickerson*, 508 U.S. 366 (1993)). Police officers can also search students who are under the power of school authorities if the search is reasonable under all other circumstances (*New Jersey v. TLO*, 469 U.S. 325 (1985)). Further, cars may be stopped and searched if a police officer has reasonable suspicion that a traffic violation has occurred or criminal activity is occurring (*Berekmer v. McCarty*, 468 U.S. 420 (1984); *United States v. Arvizu*, 534 U.S. 266 (2002)). During a traffic stop, a police officer may pat down the driver and passengers if he or she believes that any of the individuals are involved in criminal activity (*Arizona v. Johnson*, 555 U.S. 323 (2009)) and may use a narcotics dog to walk around the exterior of a car during a valid traffic stop without providing an explanation of suspicion (*Illinois v. Cabales*, 543 U.S. 405 (2005)).

Other decisions regarding search and seizure and Fourth Amendment rights provide officers the authority to search vehicles when there is probable cause to believe that the vehicle contains evidence of a criminal act (*Arizona v. Gant*, 129 S. Ct. 1710 (2009)) and at international borders, where routine stops and seizures can occur (*United States v. Montoya de Hernandez*, 473 U.S. 531 (1985)). Special law enforcement concerns, such as sobriety or seatbelt checkpoints, can be used to justify highway stops without any individualized suspicion (*Illinois v. Lidster*, 540 U.S. 419

(2004)). In *Michigan Dept. of State Police v. Sitz* (496 U.S. 444 (1990)), the U.S. Supreme Court allowed highway sobriety checkpoints for the purpose of preventing drunk driving, but the court has not allowed highway checkpoints for the sole purpose of discovery and interdiction of illegal narcotics (*City of Indianapolis v. Edmond*, 531 U.S. 32 (2000)). Finally, the Court has allowed police officers to use highway checkpoints where the stops are brief and seek voluntary cooperation in the investigation of a recent crime that has occurred on that highway (*Illinois v. Lidster*, 540 U.S. 419 (2004)).

Even though all the cases mentioned allow police officers to search without a search warrant, the U.S. Supreme Court has historically limited searches by police officers. In a recent example, the U.S. Supreme Court limited the scope of police searches when it involves a car parked around a home or on its surrounding property, known as curtilage (*Collins v. Virginia*, 524 U.S. _____ (2018)). In this case, Ryan Collins argued that his Fourth Amendments rights had been violated when law enforcement lifted a tarp exposing a stolen motorcycle on his girlfriend's property. The officers suspected that the motorcycle was stolen because Collins had twice evaded them during attempted traffic stops and had posted pictures of the motorcycle identifying its location on his Facebook page. Collins was convicted of the theft, and a lower court upheld the decision. Justice Sotomayer said, in her majority opinion, that "the lower court ruling would grant constitutional rights to people with the financial means to afford residences with garages in which to store their vehicles, but deprive people without such resources any individualized consideration as to whether the areas in which they store their vehicles qualify as curtilage" (Wheeler, 2018, para. 7). The U.S. Supreme Court also recently ruled that even if a driver of a rental car is not on the rental contract, he or she still has a reasonable expectation of privacy protected by the Fourth Amendment (*Byrd v. United States*, 528 U.S. _____ (2018)). In this case, Terrence Byrd was driving a car rented by Latasha Reed. Reed did not list Byrd as a driver for the car and was not with Byrd when he was stopped for a traffic violation. Reed had put personal belongings in the trunk of the car prior to leaving the car with Byrd. When Byrd was stopped by the police, he admitted to having a marijuana cigarette in the car. Upon learning that the car was rented and Byrd was not an authorized driver, the police searched the car and found body armor and 49 bricks of heroine in the trunk of the car. Byrd was arrested and convicted of federal drug charges. Byrd argued that it was an unlawful search and the evidence should be suppressed, but two lower courts upheld his conviction. The U.S. Supreme Court upheld the argument that a person, regardless of their status of renter

"It's a pretty nice warrant, all right, but I wouldn't call it 'outstanding'."

Source: White, A. Retrieved from http://dikenlitel.co/legal-warrant-clip-art.html.

or not, has a reasonable expectation of privacy in a home or vehicle (*Byrd v. United States*, 528 U.S. _____ (2018)). Both 2018 rulings reinforce the need for police officers to understand search warrants and to know how to obtain and complete them.

How to Obtain a Search Warrant

If the police believe they have probable cause to show a crime has occurred or is about to occur and the evidence of the crime is in a specific location or with a particular person, they can ask a judge or magistrate to issue a written search warrant. The warrant authorizes the police to search a home, car, building, or other property for evidence related to the criminal activity. The police, in some jurisdictions, must identify the exact location to be searched and provide an itemized list of items they plan to seize.

Obtaining a search warrant is preferred by prosecutors and judges as it allows for an objective review of the situation. Additionally, it can reduce the risk of evidence suppression and potential civil liability lawsuits for Fourth Amendment violations (Rutledge, 2016). When obtaining a search warrant, law enforcement officers need to understand court decisions about search and seizure, the scope of the warrant, and the rules surrounding the execution of a warrant.

Exercise 5.1

If you were requesting a search warrant for illegal narcotics at a known drug house, what items would you list on the affidavit to be seized? Name a minimum of five pieces of property you would look for during the search.

To obtain a search warrant, the law enforcement officer will typically use a standard written form, also known as an affidavit, provided by the prosecuting attorney's office or the law enforcement agency. The format may look like Figures 5.1 and 5.2. The officer will complete the form in writing and support the information provided by oath or affirmation before a judge or magistrate with jurisdiction over the location to be searched and the type of crime that is alleged to have occurred. The officer is required to demonstrate probable cause for the warrant by clearly defining the facts of the case in a way so that any reasonable officer would believe a crime has occurred or is about to occur. Included in the explanation to the judge or magistrate is a clear description of the person or location that is to be searched and the items to be seized. Once the search warrant is executed, any seized property must be brought before the court according to a timeline provided within the search warrant.

Figure 5.1   Affidavit

IN THE CIRCUIT COURT OF THE

_____ JUDICIAL CIRCUIT

_____ COUNTY, FLORIDA

STATE OF FLORIDA

COUNTY OF _____ SS

AFFIDAVIT FOR SEARCH WARRANT

Before the undersigned, _____, Judge, of the

_____ Judicial Circuit in and for the County of _____, State of

Florida, personally appeared _____, Deputy Sheriff,

_____ Sheriff's Office, who by me being first dully sworn

deposes and says:

That he/she has probable cause to believe and does believe that on the

(premises described as or in a certain building known as) 1234 Pine Street in the

City of _____, _____ County, Florida, the laws of the State of Florida

have been and are being violated. Said premise is a one (1) story cement block

structure, white with dark brown trim. The building is located on the east side

of Pine Street between Timbers Street and Third Street. The house is the fourth

house with a double car garage on the east side of the house.

Being in the City of _____, _____ County, Florida, the

laws of the State of Florida against sale, possession, or manufacture of a

Controlled Substance, Section 893.13 of the Florida State Statute, are being violated on the described premises by a person or persons unknown by reason of the following facts:

On _____, 19____, the Affiant searched a confidential informant and determined that he/she had nothing on his/her person. Affiant gave the confidential informant ten dollars ($10.00) in serialized U.S. currency with which the informant was to purchase narcotics from inside the premises so described. The confidential informant then walked directly to the entrance of the premises so described without leaving my sight, knocked on the front door, and was then observed to go inside. A few minutes later, the confidential informant exited therefrom and returned directly to your Affiant and handed to your Affiant two small manila envelopes containing about five grams of a green leafy substance in each. The informant said that these items were purchased from inside the described premises. Presumptive chemical tests were conducted on the green leafy substance and showed a positive reaction indicating the presence of marijuana THC.

A search of the described premises is to be made to seize all controlled substances, paraphernalia used in and about the possession of and sale of controlled substances, and to seize all persons in possession thereof.

Wherefore, Affiant prays that a search warrant be issued according to law commanding the Sheriff or Deputy Sheriff of _____ County, Florida, therein with proper and necessary assistance, to search the premises described and all spaces therein for the property described and to seize as evidence and to arrest any person in the unlawful possession thereof.

(*Continued*)

(Continued)

The service of said warrant is to be made in the daytime or nighttime or on Sunday as the exigencies of the occasion may demand or require.

_____

AFFIANT

SWORN AND SUBSCRIBED BEFORE ME

THIS _____ DAY OF _____ A.D. 19_____

_____

CIRCUIT JUDGE, _____ JUDICIAL CIRCUIT

The Scope of a Warrant

In general, a search warrant consists of four parts—the affidavit, the search warrant, the inventory, and the return.

The Affidavit

The affidavit is the statement of probable cause (shown in Figure 5.1). This is where the police officer requesting the warrant swears to the court that he or she has probable cause to believe a particular location or person is involved in criminal activity. The affidavit includes a description of the place or person to be searched and the items to be seized. It will also include the time of the offense and the name of the owner or person in charge of the property. In describing the place or person to be searched, police officers should include enough details so that someone unfamiliar with the location could find it or, in the case of a person, could identify him or her by description. The officer will likely include the type of construction materials (i.e., brick, concrete, metal, etc.), the color, street number, height, weight, race, gender, and other distinctive characteristics of the location or person's appearance. An example of a property description written in an affidavit may appear as such:

> The premises to be searched is a single story, single family dwelling constructed of concrete block. It is white in color and has dark brown trim. The front door of the house is painted red and faces north. A double car garage is located on the east side of the home.

The home address is 1234. These numbers are in black on the post immediately next to the front door and on the mailbox in front of the house. A six-foot tall wooden fence is painted dark brown and surrounds the back yard.

An affidavit will also include directions to the location or person. This is necessary, again, so an unfamiliar person could find the location if needed. Directions in a search warrant may read as follows:

Starting from the intersection of Main Street and Oak Avenue, proceed south on Oak Avenue about 1/2 mile to Second Street. Turn west on Second Street and travel about 1/4 mile to Pine Street. Turn south on Pine Street. Traveling south on Pine Street, the house to be searched is the fourth house on the east side of Pine Street between Timbers Street and Third Street. The house can be identified by its distinctive numbers of 1234 found on the mailbox and on the post immediately next to the front door.

If the property owner is known to the police, their name will also be included in the affidavit. If the owner's name is unknown, simply stating the residence is under the control of persons unknown is enough in the affidavit.

The Search Warrant

Following the affidavit is the search warrant (see Figure 5.2). As stated previously, the search warrant is the written order allowing police officers to search and seize the property of another. The search warrant will include the jurisdictional information as well as the order allowing the police to enter the described residence, sworn to in the affidavit, and seize the property also described in the affidavit. The search warrant will state the return date required for providing the seized evidence to the court and will order police officers to provide a copy of the warrant to the person whose property is seized. In general, search warrants are often standardized forms, much like affidavits, with only the pertinent and necessary information changed to reflect the current criminal situation.

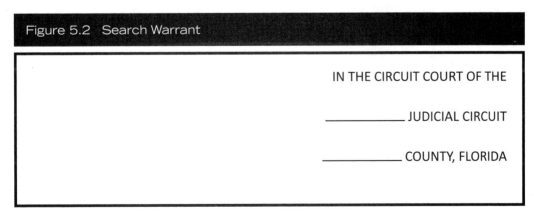

Figure 5.2   Search Warrant

IN THE CIRCUIT COURT OF THE

_____ JUDICIAL CIRCUIT

_____ COUNTY, FLORIDA

(*Continued*)

(Continued)

STATE OF FLORIDA

COUNTY OF _____ SS

SEARCH WARRANT

IN THE NAME OF THE STATE OF FLORIDA, TO ALL AND SINGULAR:

The Sheriff and/or Deputy Sheriffs of _____ County:

Whereas, complaint on oath and in writing, supported by affidavit has been before me and whereas said facts made known to me have caused me to certify and find that there is probable cause to believe that the laws of the State of Florida have been and are being violated on or in the premises known and described as follows: a one (1) story cement block structure, white with dark brown trim and bearing the number 1234 Pine Street in the City of _____, in the County of _____, State of Florida and being the premises of persons unknown, by having on and in said premises unlawful controlled substances.

Now, therefore, you with such lawful assistance as may be necessary, are hereby commanded, in the daytime or in the nighttime, to enter the said premises and then and there to search diligently for said illegal controlled substances described in this warrant, and if the same or any part thereof be found on said premises, you are hereby authorized to seize and secure the same and to make return of your doings under this warrant within ten (10) days of the date hereof, and you are likewise commanded in the event you seize or take the property and deliver a copy of this warrant to the person from whom taken or in whose possession it is found or in the absence of any such person to leave said copy in the place where said property or material was found, and you are further directed to bring all illegal controlled substances, if any found, and the person or persons in possession thereof, before me or before the Circuit Court in and for _____ County, Florida.

Witness my hand and official seal this _____ day of _____ A.D. 19____.

_____

CIRCUIT JUDGE, _____ JUDICIAL CIRCUIT

Exercise 5.2

Write a property description of your house. What details would you include so that a person unfamiliar with your home could find it?

The Inventory and Return

The inventory and return of the search warrant are included on the same written document. The inventory is a list of items seized during the search. The list will closely match the items described in the affidavit and may include things such as guns, illegal narcotics, drug paraphernalia, and any other items of evidentiary value. The return is a sworn statement that the inventory is a true and detailed account of the property seized and that the warrant has been executed. The inventory and return are signed by the officer who executed the search. A sample Inventory and Return is provided in Figure 5.3.

Figure 5.3 Inventory and Return

INVENTORY AND RETURN

RECEIVED THIS SEARCH WARRANT AT _____ COUNTY, FLORIDA,

THIS _____ DAY OF _____ A.D. 20_____.

(Continued)

(Continued)

SERVED SAME BY READING AND DELIVERING A COPY TO _____

AND MAKING SEARCH AS WITHIN DIRECTED. UPON WHICH SEARCH I FOUND:

(Provide a detailed list of the seized items here)

I, _____, THE OFFICER BY WHOM THIS WARRANT WAS

EXECUTED, DO SWEAR THAT THE ABOVE INVENTORY CONTAINS A TRUE AND

DETAILED ACCOUNT OF ALL THE PROPERTY AND APPARATUS TAKEN BY ME ON

SAID WARRANT.

SWORN AND SUBSCRIBED BEFORE ME THIS _____ DAY OF _____ A.D. 20____.

The inventory and return should be provided to the court within the timeline ordered in the search warrant.

Sworn Statements

Another way for police officers to gain evidence is through sworn statements. A sworn statement is a written statement from a person about a circumstance in which he or she was involved. Sworn statements are often obtained in writing at a crime scene during an initial investigation, but an audio or video recording of a person's testimony may also be obtained later in the investigative process.

Prosecutorial decisions, arguments made to juries, and sentencing recommendations are often made based on sworn statement testimony (Leo, 2009). Greenwood and Petersilia (1975, in Leo, 2009, p. 3) suggested that the information obtained in sworn statements "is the single most important factor in whether police will be able to solve a crime." Further, information given by victims, witnesses, and suspects both at the scene and later in follow-up investigations is a valuable resource to the court. A sworn statement serves several functions: (1) It is a recorded recollection of the victim's

Exercise 5.3

Identify three questions you would ask a witness if you were assisting him or her with writing a sworn statement. Do these questions relate to the who, what, when, where, why, or how of journalism or police report writing?

or witnesses' account of the event; (2) it can be used at a deposition or trial without the person present; (3) it can be used to refresh the testimony of a victim or witness at trial; and (4) it can be used to challenge the credibility of a victim or witness (Murgado, 2016).

Obtaining Sworn Statements

Typically, prior to writing the statement, an officer will inform the person giving the statement that providing false information is a criminal offense (Murgado, 2016). Although a police officer does not typically write the sworn statement, he or she is often the person assisting with the statement at the scene of a crime. In assisting, the police officer will ensure the statement is written in a logical format, describe the incident from beginning to end, and be understandable to anyone who tries to read it. If possible, the statement should answer the who, what, when, where, why, and how questions often used in journalistic writing and should mirror the approach used by police officers when writing police report narratives (Murgado, 2016). The officer should also ensure that the statement is factual rather than opinion based, with few sentences beginning with "I believe" or "I think." Finally, the police officer will make sure that the statement is related to the case at hand (Murgado, 2016). Keeping a victim or witness focused on what happened and his or her role in the incident is key to a useful sworn statement. Unfortunately, it may be difficult to get a victim or witness to write the statement according to these expectations since technically he or she can write whatever they want (Murgado, 2016). In the end, it is their statement. And a police officer should not coach or interfere with the information the person wants to write in the statement.

To prevent some issues with the statement, an officer will want to focus on the victim, witness, or suspect rather than multitasking (Murgado, 2016). Asking them questions to spark the facts of the case, such as what happened or what they did next, is completely appropriate as is asking if he or she is injured or if someone else was injured. The officer will also want to proofread the statement before accepting it and asking for the writer's signature. Lastly, the officer will often inform the person that proper grammar, spelling, long sentences, and so forth are not necessary, to help put the person writing the statement at ease. Doing this allows them to relax and recall the details rather than focusing on trying to impress the officer or someone else with their writing skills (or lack thereof) (Murgado, 2016).

On occasion, an officer may find that he or she has to write the sworn statement for the victim, witness, or suspect. This may occur because the person is illiterate, is traumatized by the recent events, or where English is their second language. When this happens, an officer must be especially diligent in relaying the facts in the victim's, witness', or suspect's own words.

Suspects, in particular, are protected by the Fifth Amendment of the U.S. Constitution against self-incrimination. They do not have to answer an officer's questions and may remain silent. This can include refusing to provide a sworn statement. When an officer is attempting to gain a sworn statement from a person in custody—defined as someone not free to leave or who is detained or arrested—the officer must be especially mindful of their rights under the Constitution. Before questioning this individual and accepting their statement, the officer should provide the suspect with their Miranda rights. Sworn statements under these rights should be voluntary and, like sworn statements from victims and witnesses, should not be coached or coerced by the police.

Functions of a Sworn Statement

Sworn statements, such as the one provided in Figure 5.4, can be a useful tool for police officers. Although not required under the law like search warrants, sworn statements serve many important functions. Knowing what these functions are and how to write a statement is beneficial for officers on the scene of the crime or when interviewing victims, witnesses, and suspects.

Figure 5.4   Sworn Statement

Anytown Police Department

1900 West Elm Street, Anytown USA 77750

Victim/Witness Statement Form

Case Number:_____   Date:_____

My name is _____

and I live at_____city_____state_____zip_____

My phone number is (Home)(Cell)(Other)_____

I am making the following statement concerning_____

which occurred at_____

on_____time_____A.M. or P.M.

I am making this statement voluntarily, without reward, promise of reward, threat, force, or coercion to _____

_____, a police officer with Anytown Police Department.

(Please print)_____

_____

_____

_____

_____

_____

_____

_____

_____

_____

_____

_____

_____

_____

_____

_____

_____

_____

_____

_____

_____

_____

_____(Continue on back if necessary)

Under penalties of perjury, I declare that I have made this statement of my own

free will and that the facts stated are true.

_____   _____

Signature of Victim/Witness   Signature of Officer/ID Number

CHAPTER SUMMARY

Police officers are charged with writing many types of documents. Two of the most important, mainly because they can provide evidence for court, are search warrants—which include affidavits—and sworn statements. Search warrants are generally required for all types of searches and can later be challenged in court if not written properly or with enough specificity. Search warrants and affidavits require probable cause as well as detailed descriptions of persons or places to be searched and itemized lists of property to be seized.

Since officers are often the first on the scene of a crime, they encounter victims, witnesses, and suspects. Asking these individuals to provide sworn statements is advantageous as the case progresses through the court system for several reasons. Sworn statements can be used to assist in recollection of the incident, in depositions or in court when the victim or witness cannot be present, to revive a victim's or witness' testimony, and to challenge the credibility of a victim or witness. Although police officers do not usually write sworn statements, they do play a key role in the completion of these documents and in making sure they are thorough.

QUESTIONS FOR CONSIDERATION

1. Under what circumstances can a police officer request a search warrant from a judge or magistrate?

2. What information is included in the affidavit of a search warrant?

3. What are the functions of a sworn statement?

Other Documents

Memos, Letters, Emails, Cover Letters, and Resumes

Criminal justice, like most professions, requires a lot of writing. As has been repeated many times in this book, being able to write skillfully and in a business-like manner is very important in establishing confident relationships and creating a positive image for agencies and their employees. Aside from writing job-related reports used to process criminal and civil cases, criminal justice professionals are tasked with business writing, such as memos, letters, and emails. All of these require professionalism, a business tone, proper formatting, and good English grammar. Additionally, criminal justice professionals engage in cover letter and resume writing to acquire their positions in the first place.

This chapter focuses on some universal rules and guidelines for writing various business documents and reports used by criminal justice professionals. Memos, letters, emails, and resumes will be discussed, in general.

Writing Business-Related Documents

Criminal justice professionals are required to write a number of various types of documents. The skills needed to write these documents require criminal justice professionals to be proficient in business or professional writing. Business writing is a type of professional communication. It is often called business communication and is used to convey information within and outside of agencies to specific audiences (Nordquist, 2018). The goal of business writing is to provide information quickly and clearly to the audience. Business writing is not a skill that people are born with, but it can be cultivated over time and with practice (Garner, 2013).

Business writing consists of both a style and a format or structure. Documents written in a professional style should accomplish a number of goals (Nordquist, 2018). These goals are to accomplish the following (Nordquist, 2018):

1. Convey information and/or deliver news—the document should communicate information in a clear and concise manner to the internal or external audience.

2. Direct an action and explain or justify the action—the document should tell the audience what they should do and why they should do it.

3. Influence others to take action—the document should encourage others to take the action requested or to change a policy, procedure, or in the case of for-profit companies, adopt a particular product or service.

Memos, letters, and emails are excellent choices for business writing because they allow the writer to accomplish these goals. Along with the style of writing, business writing mostly follows standard formatting rules.

In general, business documents will all look the same because standard formats are used in writing them. Using headings, dates, addresses, salutations, purpose paragraphs, and closing paragraphs are all considered part of the standard format in professional writing (Nordquist, 2018). Left justification, single spacing, and avoiding jargon are also generally accepted practices. Paragraphs are not indented in these documents. Instead adding a space between the paragraphs is sufficient for separating ideas and topics. Using everyday words, active verbs, and a conservative amount of contractions is also acceptable in formal professional writing (Nordquist, 2018). Along with a standard typeface font, like Times New Roman, writers will rely on bullets, graphs, tables, and bold face and italics when needing to emphasize important points (Gale, 2014).

Work-related writing can include memos, letters, emails, and resumes. The following sections will discuss the various types of professional documents one is likely to write when working in criminal justice.

Memos
· ·

Memos are often considered an informal means of communication; however, memos are professional documents and are used to convey very important policy or procedure information to employees. Thus, knowing how to properly write a memo and what to include in a memo is an important skill for professionals. Memos usually have eight main sections: the heading, opening, context, task, summary, discussion, closing, and attachments, if necessary (Purdue OWL, 2018c). Although the memo can follow the format provided above, the writer may place the sections in any order as long as he or she pays close attention to the readability of the memo (Purdue OWL, 2018c) In other words, the writer should write the memo in whatever order makes the most sense and is easiest to read. An example of a memo is provided in Figure 6.1.

Components of a Memo

The heading of a memo is found in list form and provides the name and title to whom the memo is written, the name and title of the person sending the memo, the date the memo is written, and the subject of the memo. Because the memo is a formal means to communicate with those holding positions higher or lower than the sender of the memo, the names and titles should be written formally, and the subject should be concise

Figure 6.1 Sample Memo

To: Ruby Smith, Chief, McCullum Police Department
From: Lamonte Jones, Assistant Chief, McCullum Police Department
Date: January 14, 2020
Subject: Body Cameras

The purpose of this memo is to explain the implementation of body cameras for all patrol officers.

The Department will begin implementation of body-worn cameras on July 1, 2020.

All officers scheduled for patrol will report to the supply office for body camera assignment at least 10 minutes before beginning a shift. The Supply Sergeant will assign and fit each officer with a body camera. The body camera should be returned to the supply office within 15 minutes of the end a shift. Body cameras should not be taken home or left in assigned patrol cars. The Supply Sergeant will ensure that all recorded information on cameras is properly downloaded to the Department server and stored. Officers should not turn off body-worn cameras during their shifts and should not delete information recorded to the cameras.

To prepare for the upcoming implementation of the body-worn cameras, please hold a staff meeting, provide training on camera policy and use, and meet with the Staff Sergeant for any additional details that may make this change easier.

If there are any questions or concerns I can assist with, please let me know. I have full confidence that our agency will make this change quickly and continue the high level of service our community expects. Thank you in advance for your continued commitment to our mission.

but specific so those reading the memo understand its' purpose (Purdue OWL, 2018c).

The opening of the memo is found in the first paragraph of the memo and will include a specific statement identifying the purpose, context, and assignment or task associated with the memo. In this paragraph, the writer of the memo will provide a brief overview of what the memo is about and express the importance of reading the memo in full (Purdue OWL, 2018c). Additionally, the opening of the memo sets the tone for the remainder of the information found in the document. The opening is typically no more than one paragraph (i.e., a minimum of three sentences) (Purdue OWL, 2018c).

The context of the memo provides the policy, procedure, or experience that is being solved by the memo. For example, the chief of police may write a memo to his or her subordinates explaining the new booking process. In the context of the memo, the writer may explain the previous task or method (how arrestees were escorted into the booking area and the paperwork required) and then state the new task or method (the new entrance process or form to be filed) to be used moving forward. Often, the context of the memo can be fully clarified in one or two sentences (Purdue OWL, 2018c).

The task of the memo builds upon the context section by describing what is being done to comply with the policy, implement the new procedure, or solve the problem (Purdue OWL, 2018c). If an action is being requested by an administrator to lower-level employees, such as police officers being asked to wear body cameras, the task section provides the space to make this request. If the memo writer is asking an administrator to make a change, the task section also provides this opportunity. In an example, a line-staff member, like a jailer, may write a memo to the police chief asking him or her to change the way inmate telephone calls are handled to better accommodate the lines that form by the phones in the local jail. Changing the line structure may increase security and decrease stress and potential arguments among inmates. This would be an important point for the line-staff member to add into the memo.

The summary of the memo is optional when compared to the other sections described. If the memo is more than one page, the summary plays an important role in re-stating the key information found in the memo. However, if the memo is brief, the summary may not be necessary. The summary may be accomplished in a single sentence, depending on its need and purpose. Lastly, the summary allows for the writer to provide reference and source information they may have used in the memo (Purdue OWL, 2018c) if these were included.

It is in the discussion of the memo that the writer provides the details that support the requests for change. The discussion section should provide the most vital information first, followed by secondary information that supports the recommendations. It is in the discussion that research or factual arguments may be introduced, with the strongest arguments coming first followed by weaker arguments (if there are any) (Purdue OWL, 2018c).

The closing of the memo should provide the reader an opportunity for further discussion and clarity. The closing should be considerate of the new actions the writer is asking someone to make or to consider (Purdue OWL, 2018c). Finally, any attachments needed to support the information in the memo can be stapled or paperclipped to the memo. The writer should refer to these attachments somewhere in the framework of the memo (Purdue OWL, 2018c).

Letters

Everyone is flooded with letters from businesses, alumni associations, marketing firms, and charities requesting donations. Many times, these letters are quickly disposed of in the closest trash can; however, letters are a very important form of communication for these groups. According to the Business Communication (2018), letters are used to sell products, make inquiries about services, build community relationships, increase goodwill, and many other functions. Letters are also used as covers (called cover letters) for resumes and applications for jobs. In criminal justice, letters are used to build relationships, communicate confidential and legal information, and to notify individuals of procedures, processes, and official expectations. Criminal justice letters are sources of proof for courts and can maintain secrecy regarding legal issues and concerns (Business Communication, 2018).

Letters in criminal justice follow the same general format described for all business communication. They are single spaced using a block font, like Times New Roman, and they use a formal tone without relying on jargon. Criminal justice letters have multiple components, just as memos, and include headings, the recipient's address, salutations, the body of the letter, the closing, and the signature line. The letters can also refer to and include attachments, if needed. Common attachments, also known as enclosures, to a business letter in criminal justice may include court orders, requests to produce documents to other parties, and/or copies of warrants, fines, or other court business. Criminal justice letters are written on agency stationery, which identifies them as a formal document and form of communication from the police department, court, or another organization.

Components of a Letter

The heading of a business letter includes the writer's name, title, address, phone number, fax number, and email address (Doyle, 2018a). If the writer is communicating on behalf of an organization or business, the writer will use the company's address as their location. The date appears after the writer's contact information. There is a double-space between the date and the recipient's information (as noted in the business letter example labeled Figure 6.2).

Immediately following the date identifying when the letter is written is the recipient's information. The recipient's information includes the formal name and title of the receiver of the letter followed by his or her address (Doyle, 2018a). If the recipient's name is not known, the sender may use a title, like President, Vice President, or Director of Communications, and the primary address of the company. The sender will double-space between the header and the recipient's information and then directly following the recipient's information include a double space again. The recipient's information is followed by the salutation.

The salutation is the greeting of the letter (Doyle, 2018a). It is always formal and begins with Dear followed by the person's name. If the gender of the person is known, the sender can put Mr., Mrs., Miss, or Ms. and the last name of the receiver after Dear—for example, Dear Mr. Jones. However, if the gender of the recipient is unknown or unclear, the sender can use both the first and last name of the recipient in the salutation. If there is a formal title for the receiver, such as Dr. or Captain, the sender can also use the title in the salutation. Examples of this would include Dear Dr. Mack or Dear Cpt. Smith. If the name of the recipient is not known, the sender can write "To Whom It May Concern:" as the salutation. This is the most formal, yet generic, salutation for unknown recipients. The salutation should be punctuated with a comma or semicolon depending on the salutation used and the formality of the letter. More formal letters require semicolons after the salutation.

The body of the letter begins after a double space behind the salutation. It is left margin justified and single spaced. Double spaces should be used between paragraphs. The body of the letter contains the nuts and bolts of the information being provided by the sender. It will state the reason for the letter and provide a more detailed explanation of what is

Figure 6.2   Sample Official Letter

Manchester Police Department
113 N. Oak Dr.
Lakeland, MN 47890

Captain Michael Jones
School Resource Officer
113 N. Oak Dr.
Lakeland, MN 47890

Parents of Fairview Elementary School
1337 Pine St.
Lakeland, MN 47890

Dear Parents,

You are receiving this letter because you have been identified as the parent or guardian of a child who attends Fairview Elementary School. Your child's school in collaboration with the Manchester Police Department will be providing a series of Kids and Technology safety programs. The programs are designed to teach parents and students how to safely use the internet, identify bogus and predatory websites, how to respond to unsolicited or malicious emails, texts, and messages, and the basics of apps and smart technology.

The one-hour training programs will be held from 6:00 p.m.–7:00 p.m. in the cafeteria of Fairview Elementary School. The first program is scheduled on May 3, 2020. Please join us!

If you have additional questions or concerns please let me know.

Sincerely,
Captain Mark Jones
Mark Jones
School Resource Officer, Fairview Elementary School

Cc: File

Enclosures

expected from the receiver, what the receiver may need to say, do, or who he or she may need to contact, and/or information about products, services, and ways to access each (Doyle, 2018a). For example, if a juvenile policing officer is informing the parents at a school of a new program for crime deterrence, the officer would provide the name, address, and phone number of the school where the program will be held in the body of the letter. The police officer would also tell the parents the name of the contact person at the school and the dates the program will be offered. The body of the letter should be formal and end with a double space prior to the close of the letter.

The final two components of an official letter include the closing and the signature line. The closing of the letter is a short statement, such as "Thank you" or "Sincerely" that signifies the letter is ending (Doyle, 2018a). The first word in the closing statement is capitalized and the closing is followed by a comma. There are usually four spaces between the closing statement and the signature line of the letter. The signature line includes the first and last name and title of the sender of the letter. For example, a female sender may write Mrs. Susan Jones, Media Communications Specialist. Additionally, the sender will sign, using cursive writing, their first and last name in the four spaces provided between the closing and signature lines.

If necessary, and enclosures are attached, a double space will follow the signature line stating "Enclosures." If no attachments are included, this word will not appear on the letter. Finally, if the letter is being shared with another party, the sender will put cc: (copy circulation) and identify the party receiving a copy of the letter. If this is noted, the receiver will know where else the letter is located and anyone else aware of the contents of the letter. An example of this is also provided in Figure 6.2, which shows the format of a formal letter.

Emails

Emails are used to communicate formally and informally. When emailing friends and family, one may use an informal tone that includes emojis and slang. The email may include incomplete sentences, lots of exclamation points, and misspellings. Conversely, when writing in one's profession, emails should be written in a formal tone. The content of the email should

"I got your email. Was it encrypted or is your spelling *that* bad?"

Source: @ Mike Baldwin; www.cartoonstock.com

be free from grammar errors and should be left justified. There should be limited use of slang, jargon, and no emojis.

Components of an Email

The layout of a formal email is similar to that of an official letter with the exception of the header. Unlike a letter, a prescribed header is not necessary. Instead of providing an official header with the sender's name, title, and address at the top of the email, the sender can place this information below the signature line. Additionally, a recognized day, time, or year does not need to be placed at the top of an email. Since an email system, like Yahoo, Google mail, or some other business software system, will generally include the sender's name, recipient's name, email addresses for both, and date, the writer does not need to provide this information in a formal way at the top of the body of the email. Instead, the email can just begin with the salutation and body paragraph. The topic of the email should be included in the subject line of the email. An email address box will automatically look like the example in Box 6.1.

Box 6.1

From: Janice Long <jlong@capebeachpd.gov>

To: Ryan Langston <rlangston@capebeachpd.gov>

Thu., 7/15/2019 4:19 PM

Subject: Draft of Body-Worn Camera Policy

If an individual is circulating a copy of the email to others, their names will appear at the top of the email in the address box as well, even if they are not actually addressed by name in the salutation of the email. In this case, the email will appear as noted in Box 6.2.

Box 6.2

From: Janice Long <jlong@capebeachpd.gov>

To: Ryan Langston <rlangston@capebeachpd.gov>

Cc: Randall Allen <rallen@capebeachpd.gov>

Thu., 7/15/2019 4:19 PM

Subject: Draft of Body-Worn Camera Policy

There is the option for a sender to blind copy circulate someone in an email (known as bcc). If this occurs, the recipient will not know this has transpired; although, the sender of the email will see the blind-copied person's name and email address in their address line (as noted in Box 6.3). It is important to always remain professional and formal in emails since one may not know who is reading the final product.

An important point to remember is that emails, like letters, can be used as evidence in court and as formal means of notification, in most states. Signature lines and signature blocks on emails have been considered legitimate authentication indicators by many state courts, and individuals can testify to the authentication of emails. Even deleted emails can be found again on Internet servers and used as court evidence. In a recent case involving a conviction of a police officer for multiple rapes, deleted emails have served as evidence in an appeal (refer to In the News 6.1). Additionally, emails can be traced from computers across Internet servers, so their authentication can be legitimized. With this said, what one sends in both formal and informal emails should not be considered private. Email is a formal means of communication, regardless of the tone of the email or from where the email is sent, and is a legally recognized way to communicate in criminal justice.

Box 6.3

From: Janice Long <jlong@capebeachfl.gov>

To: Ryan Langston <rlangston@capebeachfl.gov>

Cc: Randall Allen <rallen@capebeachfl.gov>

Bcc: Stan Cox <scox@capebeachfl.gov>

Thu., 7/15/2019 4:19 PM

Subject: Draft of Body Worn Camera Policy

Social Media

Like emails, most people consider social media an informal means of communication. However, it is used more and more by criminal justice professionals to convey information. Brevard County, Florida, for example, posts daily and weekly notices to their Facebook page on criminal activity, road closures due to vehicle wrecks, and a weekly "Wheel of Fugitive" announcement where a number of wanted individuals have their pictures placed on a wheel, the Sheriff spins the wheel, and one of them becomes the weekly most wanted offender. Other police departments do similar public service announcement postings. Just like emails, postings on social media can also be used in court and as official forms of communication. Consequently, this chapter would be remiss if postings on social media were also not discussed.

Exercise 6.1

Write a formal email and an informal email. In your opinion, when is it acceptable to send an informal email to a colleague at your agency?

Anything posted on the Internet is a reflection on an individual and, potentially, on the company or agency employing that person. Accordingly, some companies monitor social media postings by their employees and/or forbid use of the Internet and social media while employees are at work. Checking social media sites for past postings and comments is a common practice during the hiring process. CareerBuilding.com (2017) reported that more than 70% of companies use social media to screen candidates before hiring them, an increase of 50% since 2006, and over a third of companies have reprimanded or fired individuals for inappropriate comments posted on social media. Thus, posting pictures of weekend drinking habits or making comments about clients or supervisors may not bode well in a job search or once employed in criminal justice.

In the News 6.1

Oklahoma City Finds 4,000 Deleted Emails Connected to Controversy of Cop's Conviction

· ·

By Phil Cross

Daniel Holtzclaw, a former police officer in the City of Oklahoma City, was convicted and sentenced to 263 years of incarceration after a jury found him guilty of the rape and sexual assault of several women. In his appeal of the conviction, Holtzclaw argued that the DNA testing and testimony was flawed. His attorneys raised questions regarding other male DNA found in Holtzclaw's vehicle, a small sample from a victim's DNA, and DNA on Holtzclaw's pants. As a result of the appeal, more than 4,000 pages of emails and attachments were released by the Court of Criminal Appeals and Holtzclaw's attorneys tried to prevent the city from destroying even more emails related to the case.

The retired DNA Analyst, Elaine Taylor, and a police captain, Ron Bacy, had internal email exchanges regarding a news report questioning the DNA in the Holtzclaw case. Taylor sent Bacy a copy of her lab report showing that she mentioned other DNA samples and stated that it was not questioned in court by the prosecutor or defense at Holtzclaw's trial. Additionally, it was discovered that Taylor had previously emailed herself several pages from a book about forensic DNA typing and the Y chromosome and testing of the Y chromosome.

Other emails released by court order showed that the district attorney notified his prosecutors to tell him if they had pending cases where Taylor was the DNA analyst or where she endorsed the case as a witness. Emails also revealed that several other cases where Taylor was involved were marked for retesting; although, when questioned by the media the prosecutor stated that the retesting was due to Taylor's retirement not because of concerns about her work.

An independent scientist in Iowa sparked the controversy by identifying that Taylor testified that no evidence of male DNA existed in the samples but, in fact, both samples from the vehicle and his pants had other Y chromosome DNA evidence. Although, the Iowa's analyst stated that Holtzclaw could not be excluded as a contributor to the sample from his pants. The analyst stated that evidence seemed to support arguments by Holtzclaw's proponents that both samples could have come from mishandling of evidence by detectives.

Adapted from: Cross, P. (2017). Oklahoma City finds 4,000 deleted emails connected to controversy of cop's conviction. Fox 25 News. Available at http://okcfox.com/news/fox-25-investigates/oklahoma-city-finds-4000-deleted-emails-connected-to-controversy-of-cops-conviction.

For the most part, employees in criminal justice are forbidden to post formal messages to individual supervisors, subordinates, clients, or offenders on social media sites. They are, instead, required to rely on more formal means of communication, like letters and emails. Nearly all criminal justice agencies hire media experts to handle official communications from their agencies. These individuals are trained in speaking with the media, making public posts on social media sites, and in handling questions or concerns from citizens.

Cover Letters and Resumes

To get a job in the first place usually requires a cover letter and resume. This means that everyone needs to know how to write these two documents. An Internet search for both provides a plethora of information and formatting guidelines. The simplest of these rules though is to provide as much information as possible about one's skills and qualifications, to proofread the work and fix all errors, to properly format, to personalize the correspondence with names, titles, and company names of the recipients, and to follow the instructions provided by the business to apply for the wanted position (The Writing Center of Wisconsin–Madison, 2018). Cover letters are considered the first impression from the candidate and, as such, should be formal and concise.

Components of a Cover Letter

A cover letter should follow the same business communication format for letters discussed above. It should be left justified, in a formal block 12-point font, written in formal tone with little jargon or slang, and should be personalized to the person and company hiring for the job. A cover letter should be seen as the candidate's formal introduction and should provide the reason for the letter, relate his or her skills to the job's requirements, and request a meeting or discussion with the person interviewing applicants. A cover letter, like other forms of formal communication, should be written on crisp, clear, white paper and be error-free.

Cover letters should include headings, salutations, a body, and a closing. It should also indicate that a resume or application, if required, is attached (Doyle, 2018b). According to Doyle (2018b), a cover letter should include three key components:

1. A stated reason for the letter: I am applying for the position of police officer at Manchester Police Department. I have attached my resume for your review.

2. Job skills and other qualifications that relate to the job description or job advertisement: I have worked as a security officer for McMurphee Security Company for more than three years and have been trained in firearms and use of force. I also speak fluent Spanish and hold an associate degree in criminal justice.

3. Information on how you will follow up with the hiring manager and/or how you can be reached for an interview: I look forward to speaking with you about this position. I will call the Office of Human Resources to make sure my application is complete on Wednesday, June 2, 2020, *or* alternatively, I look forward to speaking with you about the position. If you need additional information, please contact me at 321-555-0101 or by email at Lmichaels@hotmail.com.

The candidate should use the cover letter to demonstrate how he or she will add to the agency, not what the agency can do for him or her (Doyle, 2018b). Additionally, the cover letter allows the candidate to show professionalism and writing skills. The cover letter is the candidate's first, and sometimes only, chance to garner the attention of the person doing the hiring, so the cover letter should be taken seriously and checked and re-checked for crucial information.

Additionally, Gallo (2014, n.p.) suggests the following when writing cover letters:

Do

- Have a strong opening statement that makes clear why you want the job and why you're right for it

- Be succinct—a hiring manager should be able to read it at a glance

- Share an accomplishment that shows you can address the challenges the employer faces

Don't

- Try to be funny—too often it falls flat

- Send a generic cover letter—customize each one for the specific job

- Go overboard with flattery—be professional and mature

Cover letters should distinguish a candidate from other job candidates but not seem fake or disingenuous by losing sight of why the candidate is applying for the position to begin with—because he or she really wants to work in this field or for this agency.

There is no need to crowd too much information on a cover letter. The cover letter should contain plenty of white space and only needs to provide three or four paragraphs, at most. Using perfumed paper or colored paper to print the cover letter is unnecessary and may actually be a distraction from the message the candidate is trying to send. Finally, the candidate should reply with a cover letter to a job advertisement in the method requested by the job advertisement. If the company asks for an emailed cover letter, then by all means one should email it. If the cover letter is requested to be hand-delivered or postal mailed, then the candidate should do that. In some cases, the job applicant may be asked to copy and paste the cover letter into an online application system. If this is the case, the candidate should still make sure the letter is formatted properly and is error free when pasted into the textbox. Along with the cover letter, a candidate may be asked to provide a resume.

Components of a Resume

Resumes are used for a variety of purposes. A person may create a resume to apply for a job, to apply for a raise or promotion, or for their annual employee evaluation. By far the most common reason a person creates a resume is to get an interview for a job (Purdue OWL, 2018d). A resume should be attached to a cover letter, if requested or required by the job advertisement. These two documents go together in the professional world.

A resume is used to present a person's skills and qualifications, background, and education for a job. A resume is not a letter, is not lengthy, and should be considered more of an outline that demonstrates a person's unique history and ability to do the job they are applying for. A resume will contain essential contact information for the candidate. This is not in the form of a formal header, like in a formal letter, but is typically centered on the top of the page and simply lists the contact information (Purdue OWL, 2018d). The contact information will include:

The candidate's full name

Address (permanent or temporary)

Phone (landline, cellular phone,
and fax number, if applicable)

Email address

Web address (if applicable)

To underscore the contact information, a candidate may choose to use a larger font for his or her name, to bold their name, and/or to use a line between the contact information and the additional information provided in the resume (Purdue OWL, 2018d). These tactics draw the interviewer's attention to the contact information. An example of this may appear as such:

LeLanna Michaels
1802 Live Oak Lane
Smithfield, Georgia 54678
Cell: 321-555-0101
Home: 321-555-9876
Lmichaels@hotmail.com

This format can be used on both the cover letter and the resume if they are presented together to the interviewer. This provides for uniformity between the two documents, presents a single professional package, and illustrates that they are from the same job applicant (Purdue OWL, 2018d).

Following the contact information, there should be subheadings that indicate the various parts of the resume. Although the subheadings may vary depending on what the purpose of the resume is (i.e., applying for a job, getting a raise or promotion, employee evaluation, etc.), a job candidate may highlight his or her education, achievements or awards, previous work experience, and skills. Candidates may also want to include an objective that identifies what they are trying to accomplish professionally. These areas are presented in Figure 6.3.

Companies will often require candidates to provide references or names of individuals who can attest to the character, work experience, and background of a job applicant. At the end of a resume, a candidate can decide if he or she should provide references for their professional and personal character. If the candidate decides to provide references, he or she should indicate so by using the subheading "References:" and then providing the names, titles, and professional contact information for the persons they have chosen to comment about their professional experience and character. If, however, a candidate decides not to provide references on the resume, the candidate can simply add "References Available Upon Request" to the bottom of the resume. This indicates to the hiring manager that there are individuals who can speak to the qualifications stated in the resume and signals that he or she should contact the candidate if they would like to speak to the references. Candidates will often use this choice if they do not want to have unnecessary phone calls made to their current or former supervisors and/or if they have not told their current supervisor that they are searching for a new position. Once the candidate is contacted for reference information, he or she can inform their current supervisor so they are alerted to the possibility of a telephone call. A candidate may also choose to use this phrase if he or she is still deciding who to ask as a character reference or if he or she needs time to contact the references before the agency does so.

The Purpose of Resumes and Cover Letters

Both resumes and cover letters introduce the candidate to the job interviewer. They should be used to highlight the most important and relevant education and skills a candidate has that relates to the position he or she is

Exercise 6.2

If you were a hiring manager, what errors would you look for in a cover letter to disqualify a candidate?

Figure 6.3 Sample Resume

LeLanna Michaels
1802 Live Oak Lane
Smithfield, Georgia 54678
Cell: 321-555-0101
Home: 321-555-9876
Email: Lmichaels@hotmail.com.

Objective:

To obtain an entry level position with Manchester Police Department that allows me to work on patrol and use my Spanish language skills.

Education:

- County Community College, Same County, MA, Associate of Science in Criminal Justice, graduated May 2018

Work Experience:

- Wilson Transportation, Driver   January 2017–Present

  Transport inmates to court, facilities, treatment centers, and halfway houses.

- McMurphee Security Company, Security Officer   August 2013–January 2017

  Secured buildings and other structures at the port, completed work logs, attended briefings and trainings, and collaborated with county and city police on investigations.

Awards and Honors:

- Dean's List, Fall 2017 and Spring 2018

- Honor Society for Criminal Justice, January 2018

- Employee of the Month, September 2017

Skills:

- Mandated State Police Certification, 2018

- Massachusetts Firearms Certification, 2014

- Georgia Firearms Certification, 2017–Present

- Fluent in Spanish

- Proficient in Microsoft Office Software

- Hardworking, dedicated, and punctual

- Great leadership skills

applying for. More detailed information on a candidate's experience can be provided once he or she is in person at the interview. When writing these documents, one should keep in mind that attention spans may be short, there may be lots of resumes to review, and the interviewer may not have a lot of time to review resumes before interviewing candidates, so keeping the resume and cover letter to a single page each is important. Longer resumes may only be acceptable if the candidate has had a lengthy career or has many special skills or qualifications related to the position. Candidates should ask themselves what it is about them that makes them uniquely qualified for the position and focus on that information in both the cover letter and resume.

CHAPTER SUMMARY

Criminal justice professionals spend much of their time writing. They are required to write professionally across many mediums, including memos, letters, emails, and, when applying for jobs or promotions, cover letters and resumes. Knowing how to write these documents and the standard formats expected in official communication is an essential skill and demonstrates a person's professionalism and abilities.

Memos and emails, although often considered informal means of communication, are legitimate communication documents and should always be treated as such. Writers of these documents should be conscientious of their purpose and the potential audience. They should also always keep in mind that these documents could be used by courts or by other criminal justice workers later to verify communications; the knowledge a person had about a policy, procedure, practice, or demand; and/or by the general public, if secured by the media or other sources. Letters, like those that may be sent from courts or probation offices, serve fundamental functions for the criminal justice system. Their tone and the information they contain may result in very serious consequences if the receiver chooses to ignore

the message. In all of the above cases, memos, emails, and letters could follow a criminal or civil case from the beginning (arrest) to the end (prison or parole). Like these more formal forms of communication, being aware of how one communicates on social media is also important.

Finally, to get a professional position in the first place, individuals have to write cover letters and resumes that stand out above other possibly suitable candidates. These documents must be able to gain the attention of hiring managers that may review many, many potential applicants. Cover letters and resumes should emphasize a person's unique qualifications for a position, while also demonstrating their professionalism and enthusiasm for the agency and job. Each one should be personalized for the position one is applying for and the company one is applying to.

To be proficient in any writing task, an individual needs to practice writing skills. A person should review templates and other examples and edit, edit, edit their own documents until just the right message is sent. A person must also constantly be careful when conveying a written message, as it is always a reflection on the writer.

QUESTIONS FOR CONSIDERATION

1. In what instances might a police officer write a memo to the department? What message might the memo contain?

2. Identify two primary differences between formal and informal emails. When is it acceptable to write an informal email to colleagues at work?

3. If you were to apply for a position as a police dispatcher, what skills or qualifications would you highlight in your cover letter? What about on the resume?

Academic Paper Formats

What Is APA Formatting?

College students are regularly asked to complete research papers in classes. The course instructor's directives for the paper probably required that students use academic formatting, most specifically American Psychological Association (APA) format. APA format is the accepted academic format for criminal justice writing. Students who become proficient in APA formatting while in college often find that they continue to use this approach when writing grants, reports, program evaluations, and other documents in their professional careers in criminal justice.

This chapter will review the necessity for APA formatting in academic projects and discuss the types of manuscripts one is likely to see utilizing APA format, ethics and legal issues in writing and publishing, and plagiarism. Other formats, the Modern Language Association of America (MLA) and the *Chicago Manual of Style (CMOS)*, will also be briefly mentioned since students may be exposed to these styles, as well.

Research, Publication, and the APA Style Rules

When someone decides to analyze data or complete a research project on a specific phenomenon, he or she becomes a researcher. That researcher's work or report may be relevant to the field of study where the phenomenon exists; thus, the researcher is expected to share the completed work with others. In doing so, the researcher expands the wealth of knowledge available to other scholars and practitioners and builds upon what is already known about a specific discipline and what may still need to be investigated. Their work provides new insight on specific phenomenon and allows others to critically assess the research, expand it, complete future projects that do not repeat the same mistakes, and contribute something new to the field of study (APA, 2010). However, in order for the work to be completely communicated to others, there has to be a standard way of writing. This is where the APA format becomes important.

The American Psychological Association created the APA format in 1929 as a method whereby researchers could formally communicate scientific research results in publications (APA, 2010). The goal was to provide a set of procedures, or style rules, that codify the format of scientific research papers to simplify reading comprehension (VandenBos, 2010). The Association has revised the APA style many times, and it often includes the input of psychologists, anthropologists, and business managers. The Association also consults with other researchers in the social and behavioral sciences when determining updates to the style. The current format (6th edition) provided by the APA was developed in consultation with the Publication Manual Task Force, APA members at professional meetings, and from APA boards and committees, which include students (APA, 2010). The style rules consist of instructions on formatting manuscripts, tables, figures, citations, and references, and the organization of papers as well as grammar and other basic information on the mechanics of writing. Some basic style guidelines from the APA manual are provided in Box 7.1 (APA, 2010).

Box 7.1
Basic Style Rules for APA Citations

APA requires resources to be cited in both the text of the document and on the last page of a document, called a reference page. APA provides very extensive citation guidelines and rules for many types of sources in their style manual. Where they do not provide a style guideline for a source, students are encouraged to choose a sample style as similar to their source as they can. Although there are no standard citation rules for all sources, some basic guidelines are provided below:

In-Text Citations

- Writers should use past verb and present perfect tenses when referring to previous research completed by authors (e.g., Smith found or Smith has found).

- In-text citations should immediately follow the sentence where the information was paraphrased and/or quoted.

- Writers should follow the author–date style when citing sources in the text of a document (e.g., Smith, 2018).

- When directly quoting from a source, writers should provide the author's last name, date of publication, and a page number—preceded by a p—from the source where the information came from (e.g., Smith, 2017, p. 135).

- Writers should place the punctuation mark after the page number or in-text citation.

- Writers should capitalize proper nouns, titles, and the first word after a colon or dash in an in-text citation.

- Writers should italicize the names of longer works if the work is used in the in-text citation instead of an author's name.

- Writers should put quotation marks around longer works in journals, television shows, song titles, and articles from edited collections.

- Writers should use special style rules for quotations that are 40 or more words that include indenting the quotation by five spaces, omitting the quotation marks, starting the quotation on a new line, and placing the page number at the end of the quotation and after the punctuation mark.

The Reference Page

- The reference list should appear at the end of the document and begin on a new page labeled "References" in the center of the page.

- Each resource cited in the document and in in-text citations should appear in the reference page.

- Writers should double-space references.

- If a reference is longer than one line, the second line should be indented 5 spaces as a hanging indentation.

(Continued)

(Continued)

- Writers should provide an author's last name first followed by the author's first initial.

- All authors up to and including seven authors should be provided in the reference. Any authors after seven should be indicated with an ellipsis.

- Writers should alphabetize the references and use chronological order for multiple articles by the same author.

- Writers should italicize longer works, like books, but not italicize, underline, or put quotation marks around shorter works, like journal articles.

- Writers should capitalize all major words in titles and provide the title in full.

- Writers should keep the punctuation and capitalization provided in a journal's name.

- Writers should capitalize the first letter in the first word of a title and subtitle, the first letter in the first word after a colon or dash, and proper nouns.

Adapted from Purdue University (2018). The Purdue online writing lab. Retrieved from https://owl.purdue.edu/.

Why Use a Style Guide?

Often, students ask why there is an emphasis on writing style versus a simple focus on grammar and proper English. VandenBos (2010, p. xiv) stated,

Uniform style helps us to cull articles quickly for key points and findings. Rules of style in scientific writing encourage full disclosure of essential information and allow us to dispense with minor distractions. Style helps us express the key elements of quantitative results, choose the graphic form that will best suit our analyses, report critical details of our research protocol, and describe individuals with accuracy and respect.

All of this clears the way for researchers to focus on the substance of their research, rather than the writing style (VandenBos, 2010).

Having a set of style rules also provides a formal system for journals, books, and other media to follow when publishing the work of researchers. Print media and digital media may require a researcher to format their work according to the APA style rules. In doing so, the work can be more easily read and reviewed by other scholars and those interested in the study. Box 7.2 provides a general guideline for information included in APA formatted references.

Additionally, legitimizing the research is a requirement of the scientific research community. This usually involves a review of the manuscript by other experts familiar with the discipline who peer-review (or referee) the paper for theory, methods, data, and analysis. The reviewers assess the strength of the project in following the scientific protocol of research. They determine the strengths and weaknesses of the manuscript, which should also be provided by the researcher in the paper, and consider the rigor of the design, methodology, analysis, interpretation of the data, and reporting. Reviewers also verify the transparency of the study's details so that others

1. Author's name(s) written with last name first, followed by first initial, middle initial

2. Year of publication in parentheses

3. Title of book, article, paper, etc.

4. Journal name italicized (omitted if not a journal)

5. Volume number of the journal or edition of the book

6. Issue number of the journal in parentheses (omitted if not a journal)

7. Page numbers where article is printed within the journal (omitted if not a journal)

8. Doi number preceded by "doi," unless it is an online journal, in which case the phrase "Retrieved from" and the URL of the website can be used

9. Geographical location (both city and state) and name of publishing company

10. End citation with a period

The APA style manual provides many other examples of citations for databases, journals, unpublished papers, interviews, social media, and so forth. Students are encouraged to purchase the most up-to-date manual early in their academic careers and to refer to it frequently when writing academic papers.

may reproduce or extend the findings (National Institutes of Health, 2017). Reviews that end in positive appraisals are published, while those manuscripts that are reviewed negatively may need to be rewritten or revised to meet the standards of the scientific community. If reviewers conclude the manuscript has serious scientific, ethical, or legal flaws, the study may never be published.

Types of Publications

Journals

If a study is published, it may appear in a journal. Students are often familiar with journals because they do online and in-person library searches for articles on various topics when writing research papers. Journals come in a variety of formats (print and digital), as well as refereed and nonrefereed. A refereed journal will use the peer-reviewed practice described above, while a nonrefereed journal may publish articles that have only been reviewed by an editor or an editorial board who may or may not have knowledge and experience related to the reviewed article's topic. In this case, the article may be reviewed more for style and formatting than for scientific and academic validity.

Scholarly or refereed journals publish articles that are considered primary or original works (APA, 2010) and may consist of "empirical studies, literature reviews, theoretical articles, methodological articles, or case studies" (p. 9). Empirical studies are original research projects that include secondary data analysis, testing hypotheses, and presentations of new data that may not have been presented in previous research studies. Literature reviews, which are most familiar to students, include synthesizing and critically evaluating previously published studies on a specific phenomenon (APA, 2010). Theoretical articles use existing publications to advance theory by reviewing the theory from development through time pointing out flaws and/or adding to or modifying the theory. Methodological articles present new methods of analysis, modify existing methods, and/or discuss quantitative and analytical approaches to data. They may rely on "highly technical materials" (APA, 2010, p. 11) and appeal to more experienced researchers. Finally, case studies are reports that illustrate a problem, provide solutions to the problem, and highlight the need for additional research on the problem, clinical applications, or theory related to the problem (APA, 2010). Other types of articles published in scholarly journals may include book reviews, letters to the editor, brief reports, program analyses, and monographs. All of these types of articles are usually refereed, or reviewed, by experts in the discipline of study. There is a plethora of these journals in criminal justice, but a few examples include *Youth and Society*, *Deviant Behavior*, *Criminal Justice and Behavior*, and *Criminology, Criminal Justice, Law & Society*.

It should also be noted that the term *journal* in the title of a publication does not necessarily indicate it is refereed (University of Washington–Tacoma, 2018). Nonrefereed or edited articles may appear in journals in print and online. Trade journals are usually considered nonrefereed or edited and are written by and for professionals in a particular field or industry. These types of journals are useful for content on current practices and programs in criminal justice and other professions (University of Washington–Tacoma, 2018). As stated previously, nonrefereed or edited journals use editors or editorial boards to review article submissions from authors. The editor or editorial board may or may not be familiar with the article's topic and typically review articles for grammar, relevance, timeliness, and style. If the article is seen as meeting the criteria, an editor can choose to publish the article in a nonrefereed journal. Although not the gold standard of publications, some articles found in edited journals are well written and contribute to the field or discipline in some meaningful way, such as those found in trade journals. However, students should not rely on these types of journals for solid, scientific content. A few examples of edited journals include *Corrections Today* and the *FBI Law Enforcement Bulletin*.

Magazines

Magazines fall into the nonrefereed or edited category. Magazines are written for a general audience and do not necessarily follow style rules, such as APA formatting. Magazines may publish articles on many topics in one edition and may have paid advertising space for various products and services. Magazines are abridged, and the determination of what to publish is decided by an editor. Articles found in magazines are assumed to be factually correct but may contain errors and be written for universal appeal rather than truth. Examples of magazines include *Police Chief*, *US News and World Report*, and *Newsweek*, among others.

Government Publications

Government publications in criminal justice tend to follow the style rules of the APA. Government publications typically are produced by the United States federal government or a foreign government. The Department of Justice publishes the majority of articles in the United States related to criminal justice, although some other departments within the federal government write articles or do studies in criminal justice too. Government publications are considered legitimate, academic (or scholarly) sources. They are reviewed by scholars in the field and undergo a rigorous editing process. Students can find government articles by searching federal government websites or using Google to search a broad topic. Google can limit the topic search to only governmental websites if *.gov* is added to the search bar. The Department of Homeland Security, Office of Juvenile Justice and Delinquency Prevention, Uniform Crime Reports, and the National Institute of Justice Publications are a few federal departments that students can use to find articles related to criminal justice topics. Of course, there are many other federal departments and websites, as well.

Books

Finally, books are often used as references in student research projects. Books are not refereed by experts in the field, though they may be reviewed by individuals with knowledge in the subject area. Typically, publishers, like SAGE Publications or McGraw-Hill Publications, commission authors to write books and guarantee the authors lump sum payments or royalties from the sale of the book. The authors may write the entire book, portions of a book, or only single chapters. Books can be used as legitimate references for research projects, but they are considered secondary sources, not primary. In most cases, students should seek primary or refereed journal articles to supplement their work and not rely solely on books.

"WHAT I CALLED CREATIVE RECYCLING THE SCHOOL CALLED PLAGIARISM."

Source: Used with permission from T- (Theresa) McCracken.

In summary, APA formatting will likely be used in almost all publications discussed in this section. APA formatting can help students decide how much authority to afford to a particular publication. If the publication follows rigid APA style and the articles in the publication are found to be refereed, the student can rest assured that the information is well-founded in scientific protocol. However, if the publication provides a mix of styles or little APA formatting, the student should likely question the contents of the work. Comprehending that APA formatting provides a way for authors to communicate ideas and research clearly to one another is significant in understanding a student's need to learn and use APA style rules. In addition to the communication goal, APA formatting plays a part in ethical and legal standards in publishing. In the next section of this chapter, ethical and legal standards are discussed in relation to APA formatting and publications.

APA Formatting and Ethical and Legal Standards

Following legal and ethical standards in writing is a requirement of scientific researchers. If a researcher fails to follow ethical guidelines set forth by the discipline, he or she may face scrutiny, the research may be disregarded, and the researcher's reputation may not recover, which would dampen future projects. Legally, a researcher is required to follow statutes governing research and, in the case of using human subjects, may have to get permission for the research from the federal office of Human Subjects Protections, the researcher's agency, or an educational institution's Institutional Review Board (IRB), which governs the legitimacy of research. Knowing and understanding these expectations is extremely important for the scholarly researcher and will be discussed in the following paragraphs.

Ethics

The *Merriam-Webster's Dictionary* (2018) defines *ethics* as a set of moral principles. It is assumed that these moral principles guide an individual's behavior by helping them to determine right from wrong. Ethics are usually learned from the family, school, in church, or in other social settings (Resnick, 2015). Groups can also have ethics or principles that guide their approach to moral issues or situations and provide a philosophy specifying how they will behave. This group philosophy is known as professional ethics when it governs behavior in a particular profession. Psychologists, doctors, police officers, and many other professions practice professional ethics. Scholarly researchers also use professional ethics founded in scientific protocol and recognized by the APA.

Just as ethics govern the behavior of professions and "establish the public's trust in the discipline" (Resnick, 2015, para. 6), ethics in research accomplishes five main goals: (1) Ethics promote knowledge, truth, and the avoidance of error; (2) ethics promote collaboration in research; (3) ethics hold researchers accountable for their work and to the public; (4) ethics build public support for the importance of research; and (5) ethics promote other social and moral causes such as human rights, legal compliance, and animal safety, to name a few (Resnick, 2015, para. 7–11). Thus, given the importance of ethics in research, it is expected that all researchers will be familiar with and adhere to the ethical standards identified within their discipline or profession and within the scientific protocol when conducting research. Typically, the researcher can find these ethical expectations in their professional code of ethics and/or on governmental websites that provide research ethics. Box 7.3 shows the professional code of ethics for police officers adopted by the International Association of Chiefs of Police in 1957. The professional code of ethics for research is provided in Table 7.1 from the National Institute of Health.

Box 7.3
Law Enforcement Code of Ethics

As a law enforcement officer, my fundamental duty is to serve the community; to safeguard lives and property; to protect the innocent against deception, the weak against oppression or intimidation and the peaceful against violence or disorder; and to respect the constitutional rights of all to liberty, equality, and justice.

I will keep my private life unsullied as an example to all and will behave in a manner that does not bring discredit to me or to my agency. I will maintain courageous calm in the face of danger, scorn or ridicule; develop self-restraint; and be constantly mindful of the welfare of others. Honest in thought and deed both in my personal and official life, I will be exemplary in obeying the law and the regulations of my department. Whatever I see or hear of a confidential nature or that is confided to me in my official capacity will be kept ever secret unless revelation is necessary in the performance of my duty.

I will never act officiously or permit personal feelings, prejudices, political beliefs,

aspirations, animosities or friendships to influence my decisions. With no compromise for crime and with relentless prosecution of criminals, I will enforce the law courteously and appropriately without fear or favor, malice or ill will, never employing unnecessary force or violence and never accepting gratuities.

I recognize the badge of my office as a symbol of public faith, and I accept it as a public trust to be held so long as I am true to the ethics of police service. I will never engage in acts of corruption or bribery, nor will I condone such acts by other police officers. I will cooperate with all legally authorized agencies and their representatives in the pursuit of justice.

I know that I alone am responsible for my own standard of professional performance and will take every reasonable opportunity to enhance and improve my level of knowledge and competence.

I will constantly strive to achieve these objectives and ideals, dedicating myself before God to my chosen profession . . . law enforcement.

Source: International Association of Chiefs of Police. (1957). Law Enforcement Code of Ethics. Retrieved from: https://www.theiacp.org/resources/law-enforcement-code-of-ethics.

Ethics in scientific protocol provides basic standards for all researchers to follow when conducting and presenting research. According to scientific protocol (Smith, 2003), when completing ethical research projects, researchers should

1. *Be truthful in discussing intellectual property.* Researchers should discuss who gets credit for the work, how authors' names will appear on projects, and what work will be done by each participant. Faculty, independent researchers, and students who share in the responsibility of contributing to the conceptualization of the project, development and completion of the project, and distribution of the research, deserve authorship and acknowledgement. Researchers also need to fulfill the ethical obligation of correcting research errors and/or allowing others to duplicate the research using the same data.

2. *Understand roles.* It is important for researchers to realize they play multiple roles in relationships. For example, a teacher who uses students in experiments may unintentionally violate the student's right to say no to the project because the student may feel pressured: If he/she doesn't participate, their grade may be affected. Research participation should be voluntary on behalf of subjects. So researchers should not take advantage of their professional role in pursuing research or research participants and should realize that the multiple roles they play in relationships with others could create a harmful or unethical environment for research.

3. *Show respect for persons.* As mentioned above, participants in research projects should do so voluntarily and without fear of harm. Research participants should know and understand the risks and benefits of the research, the purpose of the research, the expectations on their time and involvement, their ability to withdraw or refuse to participate, how their information and contributions will be identified, analyzed, and dispersed, if incentives are available for their participation, and who to contact if they experience discomfort or have questions. Researchers should get consent to participate in research in writing from subjects and should continually assess the research to ensure it is not harming participants beyond what was identified at the beginning of the project.

4. *Protect confidentiality and privacy.* Like doctors are required to secure medical records, researchers have an ethical responsibility to protect the responses and identity of those that participate in research projects. Researchers should discuss with participants how their identity will be protected and when or if their information will be shared in publications or presentations. Researchers should talk to subjects about the harms they may experience as a result of their participation and should strive to eliminate as many of those harms as possible by securing the identity of research subjects.

If a subject's name or other identifying information cannot be anonymous, the researcher should design a system to secure their data in locked cabinets or behind security passwords on electronic devices. These procedures should be shared with the subjects and their consent to participate once knowing the risk should be secured prior to involvement in the research project.

5. *Use other ethical resources.* A researcher should know and understand state and federal laws with regard to research and using human subjects in research. Additionally, a researcher should get permission for the research from their IRB if one is available or through the federal Office of Human Subjects Protections.

In addition to the ethical guidelines above, the APA requires the open sharing of data among researchers. They suggest that researchers maintain their secured data for a minimum of 5 years. This allows other researchers to request permission to view or verify the data. It also allows for questions to be answered with respect to the accuracy of the data, analysis, and publication (APA, 2010). The APA provides further guidelines on publishing data, to include duplicating work in multiple journals or articles (this should be avoided), and publishing data piecemeal or parsing out data in various publications. Accordingly, the APA prohibits researchers from misrepresenting data from its original format and publishing the same data or idea in two separate sources. The Association believes this gives "the erroneous impression that findings are more replicable than is the case or that particular conclusions are more strongly supported than is warranted by cumulative evidence" (APA, 2010, p. 13). Piecemeal publications, or unnecessarily splitting the findings across multiple articles, is also discouraged by APA because it can "be misleading if multiple reports appear to represent independent instances of data collection or analyses" (p. 14) and the scientific literature, as a whole, could be distorted. Of course, there may be times that an author must limit the amount of findings presented in a single article because of journal constraints or because the research project is ongoing. In these instances, the researchers should acknowledge any previous work using the data or idea in both the article as well as in discussions with the journal or book editor. Not doing so could result in legal as well as ethical challenges for the authors. Both copyright laws and plagiarism, which will be discussed, apply in these cases.

Discussing ethical responsibilities and understanding the potential ethical violations that may occur in a project beforehand is good practice for researchers. Being familiar with federal mandates on research ethics, like those from the National Institute of Health, manuals like the APA manual (2010), and documents like *The Belmont Report*, a 1979 report from the National Commission for the Protection of Human Subjects of Biomedical and Behavioral Research, which discussed ethical practices in using human subjects and is still the basis for ethical practices in research involving human subjects, are key in avoiding ethical violations and determining how best to handle those that may occur.

Table 7.1	Shared Values in Scientific Research
Honesty	convey information truthfully and honoring commitments
Accuracy	report findings precisely and take care to avoid errors
Efficiency	use resources wisely and avoid waste
Objectivity	let the facts speak for themselves and avoid improper bias

Source: Steneck, N. H. (2007). *ORI—Introduction to the Responsible Conduct of Research.* Washington DC, U.S. Government Printing Office, p. 3.

Notice that being truthful is an essential element of research. For those researchers that choose not to follow ethical guidelines, legal issues may arise.

Exercise 7.1

You are a student in a criminal justice class. Your professor requires a survey study of 15 undergraduate students on drug use and abuse. Since human subjects will be involved in the study, what steps or procedures should you take to ensure the protection of their rights and welfare? What are your school's IRB requirements?

Legal Aspects

Writers must also be aware of legal issues that govern publications. Copyright and fair use laws, plagiarism, and protecting the health and welfare of research subjects are some of the legal concerns that researchers must consider when completing papers, presentations, research projects, and other works. As discussed in Chapter 2, copyright and fair use laws are federal laws governed by the U.S. Copyright Office and apply to original works. You will likely recall that these statutes do not apply to ideas, facts, systems, or methods of operation. One example of a common copyright error made by students is to copy and paste charts or graphs from outside sources into their work. This is inappropriate since the chart or graph is likely copyrighted. Using the original work or paraphrasing (i.e., summarizing in their own words) the original work without giving credit to the author is a potential violation of copyright laws and could possibly result in a lawsuit by the original author. If proper credit, such as a citations and references, are provided acknowledging where the information came from, the student is typically on safe ground.

Fair use laws are a clause in the copyright law that allows nonprofit and educational institutions to reproduce original works, develop spin-offs of original works, and distribute copies of original works through sale or lease. Fair use laws also control public domain information. Public domain information includes material with expired, forfeited, or waived property rights, and where property rights do not apply, such as in government documents. Finding oneself in violation of any of the copyright laws or clauses could result in a number of legal penalties, which may include fines ranging from $200 to $150,000 for each violation, an actual dollar amount for damages, having to pay attorney fees and court fees, jail, impounding of the illegal work, and injunctions (Purdue University, n.d.). Since student writers and researchers often do not have the resources to pay fines and court costs, providing credit when credit is due is the easiest way to avoid copyright infringements. Additionally, it is an ethical requirement. Aside from civil and criminal legal ramifications, it is considered plagiarism to not provide credit to original authors.

Plagiarism

Although there are no state or federal laws against plagiarism, there can be consequences for plagiarizing and, in extreme cases, civil liability may be one result. Plagiarism is using the words or ideas of another without affording proper credit to the original author. The APA Ethics Code Standard 8.11, Plagiarism, forbids authors from claiming the words or ideas of another as their own (APA, 2010). Using only a few words, full sentences, or entire works in a paper or presentation without affording the original author the credit makes it appear that the writer created the work. This is an example of plagiarism. Self-plagiarism is also unethical and includes using previously published or submitted work as new scholarship. For example, a student who submits a paper in one class that was already submitted and graded in another class commits self-plagiarism. In yet another example, an author who submits a previously published article to a different journal has committed self-plagiarism. To avoid self-plagiarism "the core of the new document must constitute an original contribution to the knowledge, and only the amount of previously published material necessary to understand that contribution should be included [in the new work]" (APA, 2010, p. 16). Additionally, when using previously published or submitted work, the author's own words should be cited, and references should be made to the fact that the work was used previously. The writer should say things like "as I stated previously" or "as I published previously" to inform the readers that the material has been used before. The writer should also provide in-text citations that include his or her own name and the date the previous paper or article was published or submitted.

Committing plagiarism can result in hefty consequences. In 2003, a news reporter from the *New York Times*, Jayson Blair, was accused of plagiarizing 36 of the 73 articles he wrote for the newspaper. He copied words or stories from other news outlets, faked photos, committed self-plagiarism, and made up facts and quotes in many of the stories (CNN.com, 2003). As a result of his transgressions, he was fired from the newspaper and a very public investigation and article appeared in the paper describing what he had done. Blair has never worked in journalism again (CNN.com, 2003). Other cases of plagiarism have resulted in similar fates for journalists and book authors. One book author, Kaavya Viswanathan, was accused of plagiarizing portions of her book from other authors in the same genre and had a book deal worth more than half a million dollars revoked (Bailey, 2012). Viswanathan also changed careers as a result of the accusations. Students in college who commit plagiarism may also face severe penalties that include zero grades on papers or projects, referrals to academic dishonesty investigatory boards within the university, failing a class, and/or expulsion from the university, depending on the severity of the plagiarism. Box 7.4 demonstrates Harvard University's student code of conduct with regard to plagiarism. Notice that the university refers to plagiarism as academic dishonesty and places the responsibility for upholding academic integrity upon

Box 7.4
Harvard University's Tips to Avoid Plagiarism

Writers are required to differentiate their own words from those of others. They are required to format papers in such a way that a reader can identify a source used by the writer and to format information according to standard style rules. These style rules include APA, MLA, or *Chicago Manual of Style* guidelines.

It is considered plagiarism if a writer fails to acknowledge the work of another, claims—intentionally or unintentionally—the words or ideas of another, incorporates facts from another's work, or uses language written by another without providing the proper credit to the original author (Harvard Extension School, 2017–2018). Plagiarism in an academic environment can result in very serious consequences.

The University of Harvard places responsibility for avoiding and for identifying plagiarism on both faculty and students. Students are responsible for knowing and understanding the policies on academic integrity and for using sources in responsible ways. Harvard does not provide leniency for students who claim not to understand the rules and for those that "fail to uphold academic integrity" (Harvard Extension School, 2017–2018). Faculty are also responsible for paying close attention to work submitted by students and reporting violations of academic integrity and cheating to the dean of students.

Harvard, like many other schools, provides failing course grades for students who violate cheating and plagiarism policies. They may also suspend students for one academic year.

According to the Harvard Extension School (2017–2018), students can use the following tips to avoid plagiarism:

1. Cite all sources—this includes primary and secondary sources as well as online, open source, and instructor lectures.

2. Make sure to understand the assignment and its requirements—make sure the instructor wants outside sources to be included in the assignment and make sure to use the proper citation style

3. Do not procrastinate—waiting to the last minute to complete the assignment may allow for citation mistakes to occur. Work ahead and take the time necessary to avoid plagiarism.

4. Make sure to include all sources and be thorough—even when writing draft assignments, be sure to include all sources used to paraphrase, draw ideas, and quote. Put sources into the paper and the bibliography as it is written, not at the end.

5. Use your own words as much as possible—rather than rely on quotes and the words of others, students should "actively engage with the [intellectual] material" rather than stringing together long quotes from other scholars (Harvard Extension School, 2017–2018).

Source: Adapted from Harvard Extension School (2017–2018). Tips to avoid plagiarism. Harvard University. Available at https://www.extension.harvard.edu/resources-policies/resources/tips-avoid-plagiarism.

the student. This is common practice for all writers, regardless of status (i.e., researchers, faculty, authors, students, etc.). It is the author, not the publisher, who is responsible for avoiding plagiarism.

The Protection of Human Subjects

Finally, a legal issue confronting researchers is the protection of human subjects. The APA requires researchers to meet certain ethical requirements when using human subjects in research projects. These guidelines include the following:

1. Seeking university approval for the study

2. Getting informed consent from research subjects to participate in the study

3. Obtaining informed consent for recording voices or using images in the study

4. Taking steps to prevent individuals who withdraw or refuse to participate and protecting those that are clients, subordinates, and student participants

5. Only failing to use informed consent when certain factors are met (i.e., data collection is anonymous, where no harm or distress is involved for participants, and where no federal, legal, or institutional regulations exist)

6. Avoiding offering excessive inducements to coerce research participation

7. Avoiding deception in the research, especially if there is the potential for harm or distress for human subjects

8. Providing a debriefing for participants

9. Humanely providing, caring for, and disposing of any animals that participate in research studies (APA, 2018)

APA format suggests that authors include descriptions of how they accomplished these guidelines in any papers or presentations resulting from their studies. Additionally, the Association suggests that protecting the confidentiality of research participants is the primary responsibility of the researcher. To protect confidentiality, the researcher should avoid "disclosing confidential, personally identifiable information concerning their patients, individual or organizational clients, students, research participants, or other recipients of their services" (APA Ethics Code Standard 4.07, Use of Confidential Information for Didactic or Other Purposes, 2018). To protect confidentiality, a researcher can allow the participant to read and consent to the written material once the data have been analyzed and summarized and/or the researcher can disguise some aspect of the participant, such as changing their name, altering characteristics, limiting descriptions of characteristics, using composites, or adding extraneous information to the descriptions (APA, 2010, p. 17).

Additional methods of protecting human subjects are provided by educational institutions and government entities that play a part in research that uses human participants. These bodies mandate IRBs that provide for the ethical and regulatory oversight of research projects. IRBs have the ability to approve, make modifications to, and reject research proposals that involve human subject participation. Fundamental in their role is to ensure that human subjects are humanely treated and that their rights and welfare are protected during the study's duration. The IRB reviews research protocol and other materials prior to the beginning of the study and before any humans participate to make their determinations regarding appropriateness. Legal mandates, like those published in the Federal Register (2018), require IRB reviews for studies funded by federal agencies. Universities, although not federally mandated to have IRBs unless they participate in federally funded research, usually require students and faculty to seek IRB approval before participating in projects involving human subjects. Not doing so can result in sanctions for the student and/or faculty member and, in the case of funded research, revocation of the funding and termination of the research project. Thus, researchers planning a study using human participants should become familiar with their institution's IRB standards and review procedures.

Typically, the review process is similar across all institutions and includes an application, a review, and a decision. The application asks researchers to identify the research project, hypothesis, methods, and methodology, as well as specific characteristics about the human subjects to be recruited, their participation expectations, harms, duress, rewards, and debriefing procedures. Other questions and documents, like the informed consent forms, may be required with the application and used to determine if the rights and welfare of the subjects are protected (Federal Register, 2018). If the researcher is not using protected groups, such as prisoners, pregnant women, children, in vitro fertilization, or mentally incompetent persons, the IRB may choose to use an expedited review process where only one or two members of the board review the application and make a decision. If, however, protected groups are being recruited for the study, a full board review will be required before a decision can be made to approve, modify, or disapprove of the research application (Federal Register, 2018). The review process can take several months, so researchers should consider this when preparing to complete a research study.

In summary, research is guided not only by the ethical standards developed by the APA, but also by legal and ethical expectations set by the federal government and educational institutions. Students in criminal justice are expected to know and understand the importance of using a uniform style of writing to present research and to follow the "sound and rigorous standards of scientific communication" (APA, 2010, p. xiii). The APA sets this style and provides a format, or simple set of rules (e.g., style rules), to facilitate reading comprehension in the social and behavioral sciences. Found in the *Publication Manual of the American Psychological Association,* the style rules provide a model of writing across many social science disciplines and bring together the diverse approaches and scholarship for the benefit of readers and scientific literature, in general.

Modern Language Association and the *Chicago Manual of Style*

This chapter would be remiss if two additional styles of writing were not mentioned, albeit briefly. As discussed in detail above, the APA format is the most widely accepted style in social and behavioral science writing; however, two other styles of writing are sometimes used in journals, magazines, and at educational institutions. These styles include the MLA and the *CMOS*.

Modern Language Association

The MLA was founded in 1883 and is the most frequently used formatting style in the humanities and liberal arts (MLA, 2018). The MLA hosts national conferences and an informative website for style rules and formatting. With more than 25,000 members, the MLA has worked to "strengthen the study and teaching of language and literature" (MLA, 2018, no page). Like APA format, the MLA has established writing guidelines for formatting, page layout, abbreviations, footnotes, quotations, citations, and preparing manuscripts for publication. It also includes guidelines for plagiarism. Unlike APA format, which provides very specific style rules for almost every type of source in a lengthy manual, the MLA uses a core elements approach to citing sources. In this approach, writers only need to identify nine elements in each source. These include

1. Author
2. Title of source
3. Title of container
4. Other contributors
5. Version
6. Number
7. Publisher
8. Publication date
9. Location (MLA, 2018)

Once the writer has identified these core elements, he or she can use this format for basically any type of resource. If the source is a smaller work inside of a larger work (i.e., a poem in a book of poetry), the writer should consider the smaller work (poem) the source, while the larger work (book of poetry) is the container. The container is identified in the core elements as is the smaller work. Those interested in MLA style format can visit the MLA website at www.mla.org for more information.

Exercise 7.2

What would you do if you knew a student in your class was selling papers to other students to submit for grades in a course. Is this an ethical or legal violation? Why or why not? Since you know of the infraction, can you be held accountable if you choose not to do anything?

Chicago Manual of Style

Last, but certainly not least, is *CMOS*. This style of writing is normally used in history and a few social sciences. This style uses two formats when citing resources. The first is the notes and bibliography (NB) system, which relies on footnotes and endnotes to create references to sources used in papers. In this system, the quote or paraphrase is numbered, and the corresponding number is placed at the end of the page or within a list of references with the full information needed to locate the source. The second system is an author–date (AD) system, where the author's name is found first in a reference and the date is placed last in the reference. More information on the systems used by *CMOS* can be found in the manual or online at www .chicagomanualofstyle.org/home.html.

The main differences in the three styles of writing—APA, MLA, and the *CMOS*—is where the emphasis is placed on citing sources and references and which disciplines use the style. APA format is most commonly used in the social sciences and places emphasis on the date the work was created. The date of publication is placed in in-text citations immediately following the quote or paraphrase and immediately after the author's name in the references. The most recent style rules for APA format can be found in the newest edition of the *Publication Manual* (Angeli et al., 2010) on the APA website at www.apastyle.org/ and on the Purdue OWL: APA Formatting and Style Guide at https://owl.purdue.edu/owl/research_and_citation/apa_style/ apa_formatting_and_style_guide/general_format.html. MLA is primarily used in the humanities and liberal arts and emphasizes the authorship of the work. The author's name is placed in in-text citations in the body of the paper, and the author's name is found first in the references section of the paper. MLA uses core elements to format citations that apply to almost any type of source. The formatting can be found in the newest edition of the MLA manual (Angeli et al., 2010). Last, *CMOS* is used by some social sciences, but mostly in history. The *CMOS* uses two types of citation and reference styles: a notes and bibliography system and an author–date system. The notes style is generally used by history and relies on footnotes and endnotes when citing sources. The *CMOS* latest guidelines can be found in the manual (Angeli et al., 2010). Even though there are multiple formats of writing, students in criminal justice use APA formatting and follow the ethical and legal standards put forth by the APA *Publication Manual*, universities, and federal mandates.

CHAPTER SUMMARY

Regardless of the writing system used, formatting and writing style are important to simplify the writing process for the author and to make things easier for the reader. By following standard guidelines in writing, authors within disciplines can more easily create and publish works for general consumption and for use in academic scholarship. The rules in which they design their research are agreed upon by all within the discipline so researchers can focus on the essence of the research. Thanks to style rules, readers can effortlessly identify sources within written documents and can read for understanding rather than worrying about the style rules of grammar, citation, referencing, graphing, and so forth. In the social sciences, particularly criminal justice, the APA sets the style rules followed by researchers, writers, and publishers.

In addition to general style rules, the Association provides guiding principles in research and writing ethics. Federal government offices provide legal mandates on research, and universities comply with both the ethical and legal standards by reviewing and ensuring that students and faculty are following the laws, protecting human subjects, and providing credit for works used in their investigations. Individuals found to violate the ethical or legal directives may find that they experience civil or criminal penalties and/or are ruined as writers, authors, or researchers.

QUESTIONS FOR CONSIDERATION

1. Identify the most pressing ethical issue in social science research, in your opinion.

2. Identify an ethical violation commonly committed by students at a university. Why is this behavior unethical?

The Academic Research Paper

Many students cringe at the very thought of writing a research paper. It is often viewed both by strong writers and those who lack confidence in their writing skills as a tedious, boring assignment that requires a great deal of time to complete. This chapter will introduce students to conducting research, locating and evaluating sources, reading scholarly journal articles, and writing a research paper using credible sources. The appendix also includes a sample student essay. With the guidance contained in this chapter, students should no longer dread a research paper assignment.

The Research Writing Process

The research paper is similar to other kinds of essays, "the difference being the use of documented source material to support, illustrate, or explain" the writer's ideas (Wyrick, 2013, p. 371). It is "a documented essay containing citations to the source you have consulted (that) combines your own ideas, experiences, and attitudes with supporting information provided by other sources" (Schiffhorst & Schell, 1991, p. 325). Readers may also find your resources useful to their research of similar topics.

Create a Realistic Schedule

Writing well takes time, so plan your time well. Always begin by setting a realistic schedule for completing the essay, taking account for the responsibilities and activities in your life such as other classes and assignments, home life, work, and social time. Consult the course syllabus and review the course policies for submitting assignments. Many professors will not accept late submissions or significantly lower the grade for late work. It is always safest to treat the assignment due date as an absolute deadline with no option for submitting the paper late.

Students will usually have several weeks to complete an essay assignment, but do not fall into the procrastination trap by putting things off that are not immediately due. Start planning and brainstorming topic ideas as soon as the assignment is received. Allow time for brainstorming, researching, drafting, and revising, revising, revising, and pay close attention to drafts or other assignments due before the research essay's final due date.

Finally, print or create a paper copy of the schedule and post it in a conspicuous place to serve as a constant reminder. A sample schedule based on a five-page research essay is shown in Table 8.1.

Table 8.1 Sample Paper-Planning Schedule

Task	Required Time	Due Date
Research essay assignment received from professor		Assigned on Aug. 20
Brainstorm topic ideas	1 hour	
Quick Internet search to ensure source material is readily available	1 hour	
Research	3 hours (minimum—more for longer assignments)	
Writing, Rough Draft 1	5 hours	
Submit Draft 1		**Due Sept. 3**
Writing, Rough Draft 2	3 hours	
Submit Draft 2		**Due Sept. 10**
Research	2 hours	
Writing, create references page	1 hour	
Writing, final draft and editing	3 hours	
Submit Final Research Essay		**Sept. 16**
Total time based on a five-page essay	19 hours	

Select a Topic

A professor may assign the research essay topic, or a student may be free to select a topic. One way to make the research essay assignment more satisfying for the writer and interesting for the reader is to write about a familiar topic. "The best way to avoid . . . needless drudgery is to choose a subject you already know something about and want to learn more about" (Schiffhorst & Schell, 1991, p. 327). Consider choosing "something that interests you. You'll be spending a lot of time on this assignment, and you'll be happier writing about a topic that engages you" (Brown, 2014, p. 244). Take the time to fully explore the choices, making certain the topic satisfies the requirements of the assignment. It is always best to check with the professor for additional insight and final approval.

Focus on the Topic

Inexperienced writers often choose an essay topic that lacks focus. If a student were to research police body cameras, from example, it would be impossible to read and evaluate the information contained in the thousands of websites, journal articles, and databases that would be discovered.

Before beginning the research, develop some specific ideas on what the audience should know about the topic. An essay on police body cameras might address one of these more focused concepts:

1. Do police body cameras reduce use of excessive force incidents?

2. What is the effect of body cameras on community relations?

3. Can the use of body cameras reduce the number of misconduct complaints?

4. Is a citizen's right to privacy violated by the use of body cameras?

5. Can the use of body cameras increase the safety of officers and the public?

When considering a topic, make certain a sufficient body of literature exists to support your thesis. While an abundance of information about police body cameras can be easily located, little has been written about police accreditation. Despite its interest to the writer, choosing a topic without easily available and adequate resources will make researching and writing the research paper especially difficult.

Exercise 8.1

Each of the topic questions listed below are too broad for a research essay assignment. For each, list two or three ideas on how these topics could be focused into a more appropriate essay topic.

1. Do police officers use too much force?

2. Does segregation really protect inmates from violence?

3. Should all juveniles who commit a felony be charged as an adult?

4. What challenges does a felon face when seeking employment?

Locating Sources

Primary and Secondary Sources

Primary sources include research, publications, reports, interviews, and other original material (Schiffhorst & Schell, 1991). Secondary sources are created with the support of primary sources. Primary sources give a truer sense of the topic than any secondary source could provide (Bombaro, 2012). Collecting data from a primary source, though, can be challenging. Obtaining primary source data requires conducting individual or focus group interviews, completing survey research, or observing participant behavior, and the process can be both costly and time-consuming. Some primary source data collected by researchers are available on criminal justice databases. For example, a student researching family violence might consult a Bureau of Justice Statistics (BJS) report. The report is a primary source since it is based on crime statistics collected and analyzed by the BJS, and this information is essential to understanding the issue. Students should "locate and use as many primary sources as possible" (Schiffhorst & Schell, 1991, p. 336).

Secondary sources rely on interpreting primary or other secondary sources to support or counter the author's thesis. These include books, scholarly articles, and other documents authored by someone who did not conduct original research or experience the event first-hand (Brown, 2014). Students should evaluate secondary sources carefully for credibility. Companies and organizations often fund research with the intent of a predetermined outcome. Information about evaluating sources is included later in this chapter.

General Search Engines

The Internet is an important resource and should be a part of your research plan. With just a few keystrokes, a seemingly endless collection of information can be located. Google, Bing, and Ask are the most popular general search engines, but students should always be cautious of Internet information since anyone can post information to the Web (Ratcliff, 2018).

Search engines seek matches to search terms by scanning millions of Web pages (Hacker, 2006). General search engines can be a good starting point for research, and even Wikipedia can identify valuable source information. But general search engines should not be used as a primary source for information. Later in this chapter, we discuss evaluating the credibility of sources.

Utilizing Search Parameters

Use search parameters to refine and focus a search.

1. Use quotation marks around words to search for an exact phrase: "police use of force."

2. Put a dash (–) in front of words that should not appear in the results. If a search were conducted for police but not sheriff, this would appear as police – sheriff. **

3. Use OR if either of two terms should appear in the results: police or sheriff.

4. Insert "site:" in front of a word to search for websites or domains: Site: corrections.

Many search engines have an Advanced Search page for other search options. Google, for example, includes the following page to help focus a search:

Advanced Search		
Find pages with...		**To do this in the search box**
all these words:		Type the important words: tricolor rat terrier
this exact word or phrase:		Put exact words in quotes: "rat terrier"
any of these words:		Type OR between all the words you want: miniature OR standard
none of these words:		Put a minus sign just before words you don't want: -rodent, -"Jack Russell"
numbers ranging from:	to	Put 2 periods between the numbers and add a unit of measure: 10..35 lb, $300..$500, 2010..2011
Then narrow your results by...		
language:	any language	Find pages in the language you select.
region:	any region	Find pages published in a particular region.
last update:	anytime	Find pages updated within the time you specify.
site or domain:		Search one site (like wikipedia.org) or limit your results to a domain like .edu, .org or .gov
terms appearing:	anywhere in the page	Search for terms in the whole page, page title, or web address, or links to the page you're looking for.
SafeSearch:	Show most relevant results	Tell SafeSearch whether to filter sexually explicit content.
file type:	any format	Find pages in the format you prefer.
usage rights:	not filtered by license	Find pages you are free to use yourself.

Advanced Search

Source: Google and the Google logo are registered trademarks of Google LLC. Used with permission.

Google Scholar

Google Scholar (GS) can help focus a search since it omits general readership returns. Google describes the site as "a simple way to broadly search for scholarly literature . . . (such as) articles, theses, books, abstracts and court opinions, from academic publishers, professional societies, online repositories, universities and other web sites" (Google Scholar, n.d.). Anyone who knows how to use Google can effectively use GS to quickly access research articles completed by scholarly authors. Like any product, though, GS is not without criticism. Shultz (2007) suggests the advanced search function can be unreliable and that some returns may not be scholarly. Like any source, GS should be used cautiously by the researcher, and materials should be evaluated critically. GS should never be the sole source of identifying research materials, and it should never replace library databases. Nevertheless, GS can be an effective starting point for students to identify scholarly materials and authors. Cathcart and Roberts (2006) suggest GS is but one database and is best used "as a bridge to the more reliable, comprehensive resources offered by the libraries" (p. 14).

1. What name do the British use for the American Revolutionary War?

   Search: site: uk American Revolutionary War

2. What was the Russian name for the war on the eastern front in WWII?

   Search: site: ru wwII eastern front

3. How is gun ownership reported by United Kingdom and American news outlets?

   Search: site: uk US gun ownership, site: us gun ownership

See answers on p. 147.

Utilizing Country Codes

According to Alan November (2016), the challenge of Internet research is in "learning how to access and synthesize massive amounts of information from all over the world. To manage overwhelming amounts of information, it is critical to learn how to design searches that take you past the first page of results" (para. 8).

Google's default setting is to search websites in the region where the search originates. Whenever a student researches a problem that involves another country, they should use a country code to generate sources from that country (November, 2016). For example, perhaps a student wants to research differences in police use of force between the United States and the United Kingdom. Using the search terms "use of force" and "differences in US and UK policy" returns few results. But adding the search term "site:" and the country code UK (site: uk) focuses the search to UK sources and provides insightful information that might not otherwise be found. Adding "ac" to the search term, such as site: ac.uk, limits results to UK academic institutions. A list of country codes can be found at www.web-l.com/country-codes/.

Utilizing Databases

Criminal Justice Databases

Criminal justice databases focus on issues related to crime, prisons and jails, probation and parole, juvenile justice, and the courts. The information located in these databases comes from journals, books, and government reports. Use these and other related databases when researching a criminal justice topic.

1. National Criminal Justice Reference Service: www.ncjrs.gov/index.html

2. National Archive of Criminal Justice Data: www.icpsr.umich.edu/icpsrweb/content/NACJD/index.html

3. Bureau of Justice Statistics: www.bjs.gov/

4. Federal Bureau of Investigations Publications: https://ucr.fbi.gov/ucr-publications

5. Criminal Justice Abstracts (Access through an institution or local library. See Library Databases.)

6. Journal Storage (JSTOR): www.jstor.org/

Students can find an extensive listing of criminal justice databases compiled by the University of Michigan at http://libguides.umflint.edu/c.php?g=428962&p=3263967.

Library Databases

Some databases charge a subscription fee and are not as straightforward to access as general search engines. Most college libraries and some public libraries subscribe to databases that provide unlimited access to scholarly resources not available on the Internet (Hacker, 2006). Databases like Pro-Quest, EBSCO*host*, and LexisNexis fall into this category. Check the Library website or ask a librarian about how to access these sites.

LexisNexis Academic

The LexisNexis database contains information collected from thousands of legal and news sources. Full-text publications are available from newspapers, legal news, magazines, medical journals, trade publications, transcripts, wire service reports, government publications, law reviews, and reference works (LexisNexis, n.d.). LexisNexis Academic is available only by subscription.

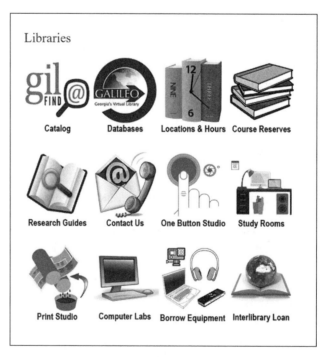

Source: Abraham Baldwin Agricultural College Libraries. http://www.abac.edu/academics/baldwin-library.

Procon.org

ProCon.org describes itself as a nonprofit nonpartisan public charity (that) provides professionally researched pro, con, and related information on more than 50 controversial issues . . . by presenting controversial issues in a straightforward, nonpartisan, and primarily pro-con format (ProCon, 2019). Students who struggle with selecting a topic will find the site's broad selection of timely and relevant issues to be an excellent starting point for the research paper.

Topics are introduced with a thorough summary followed by an easy-to-read, side-by-side debate of both sides of the issue. The site notes, for example, that police body cameras may improve officer accountability, while acknowledging the cameras may invade the privacy of citizens (ProCon 2019). Source information is well documented, and facts can be evaluated for accuracy.

Traditional News Sources

Although print and traditional TV news outlets have faded in popularity, newspapers and network channel news sources remain valuable sources of information for researchers. EBSCO, a leading provider of databases and information sources to libraries, provides access to full-text newspapers covering national and international events (EBSCO, 2018). Transcripts from television and radio news casts are also available. Many college and university libraries subscribe to EBSCO*host*, where students can access "nearly 60 full-text national and international newspapers and more than 320 full-text regional newspapers" (EBSCO, 2018, para. 3).

Benefit From Previous Research in the Topic Area

Students can benefit from the work of authors who have studied and published research similar to their topic. When a source is located, students should carefully read the reference page, paying particular attention to titles that appear to be closely related to their topic. The bibliographic information should be added to the working bibliography. Using the author's name and title of the work, search one of the earlier described database until the source is located. It is always best to locate a full-text copy of the source. Students can read the full details of the work and evaluate its usefulness to their research essay.

Evaluating Sources

All source material should be evaluated thoroughly since anyone can post information to the Web. Using an implausible source can discredit an essay and the writer. According to Kirszner and Mandell (2011), students should ask four questions when evaluating sources:

1. Is the source *respected*? Peer-reviewed scholarly articles are valued much more than general readership articles. Likewise, a major news publication, like the *Wall Street Journal* or the *New York Times*,

is considered a more dependable source than an independent newspaper.

2. Is the source *reliable*? Reliable sources depend on factual, documented information that supports the thesis. In a reliable source, the author will include source citations that can be checked for accuracy.

3. Is the source *current*? Current sources provide information relevant to the topic. There is no standard for how old a publication might be yet still remain current. A technology article could be outdated in a year or less, while information on community policing from the 1980s might be current.

4. Is the author of the source *credible*? What other publications has the author written, and have they been cited by other researchers? Is the author employed by company or foundation that suggests a particular bias? (pp. 760–761)

The use of credible sources is a sign of a well-written essay.

How to Read a Scholarly Article

Critically reading a scholarly article can be challenging for students. Even for students who are strong readers, the scholarly article is unique from other writing genres. The format, language, and data tables make it an "active, complex process of making meaning in which a reader draws information from several sources and concurrently constructs a representation of a text's message" (McLoughlin, 1995, p. 29).

Scholarly articles follow a specific format that includes an abstract, introduction, literature review, research methods, analysis, findings or results, discussion, and references. The abstract appears at the beginning of the article and is usually limited to about 250 words. It is a summary of the problem examined by the author, an overview of the study, and the author's findings. The introduction identifies the need for research in the topic area, identifies the focus of the study and its relevance to the field, such as criminology. To fully understand the issue, a literature review is included, which is the author's research in the topic area. The literature review is described in more detail later in this chapter. The research methods section includes information about critical aspects of the study: the data, the research sample, and a description of the statistical or other methods used to analyze the data. First, it is important to understand the source of the type of data to be analyzed. Are the data qualitative or quantitative? Qualitative data are numbers, while quantitative data are text, such as subject interviews and observations of study subjects. Is the author using primary or secondary data, and how were the data collected? Next, it is critical to understand the unit of analysis. In other words, what exactly is the researcher analyzing: individual people, groups, criminal justice agencies or programs, or other outcome measures? Virtually, anything can be analyzed. Finally, what methods did the author use in the analysis? The analysis section is often the most difficult for students to comprehend. In this section, the researcher reports in detail the application of statistical methods or other means of data analysis and the outcomes of the data analysis. Charts, graphs, and other visual representation of the analysis are included in this section. In the findings or results section, the author interprets the results of the data analysis. In this section, the researcher applies the outcome of the analysis to the research questions and determines if the analysis supports or refutes those questions. Finally, the author summarizes the study in the discussion section. Researchers often discuss the limitations of the study, if the findings add to the scientific literature in the field, and the need for future studies in similar areas not included in the study.

Successful students often employ a strategy when reading scholarly articles rather than using an approach similar to other reading assignments. If an English professor assigns Nathaniel Hawthorne's *The Scarlet Letter*, the most efficient approach to reading the text is to start at the beginning and continue straight through to the end. But this approach is often not the most effective way to the read a scholarly article. Students should first read the title, abstract, and discussion. This will help the student determine the nature of the study, what the author intended to prove, and if the study was successful toward that end. Next, skim the literature review, research methods, and analysis to understand how the study was conducted. Then reread the results and discussion sections closely. Students should then scan the references section to identify other studies that may benefit their research. Lastly, students should make brief notes or annotations while reading the scholarly article with a particular focus on areas that might be useful to their research.

Not every published article is written well, and it is highly unlikely that every study discovered and read by a student will be valuable to the research at hand. With some practice, though, this reading strategy will help students understand the scholarly article and decide if it can add value to their study.

Writing a Literature Review
• •

Scholarly articles and essays written for graduate-level criminal justice courses require the inclusion of a literature review. Professors who teach undergraduate courses may require a literature review as well. The literature review is a summary of what the literature says about a specific topic (Purdue OWL, 2018b). It is essential for a writer to understand the topic, theoretical perspectives, problems in researching the topic, and major controversies in the topic area of any research project (Adams, Kahn, Raeside, & White, 2007). Reading as much of the available literature as possible is the only way to do this.

The abundance of literature in any topic area requires students to narrow the topic and focus the research questions so that identified literature in the topic area is itself as limited and focused as possible. That said, a search in most topic areas will return an abundance of potential sources. Reading source material will increase the student's knowledge in the topic area and lead to other potential source material. When reading, students should identify experts in the field and seek out their literature in the topic area. Reading will also reveal theoretical perspectives used to identify the type of data needed to answer the research questions (Adams et al., 2007). Additionally, problems with researching the topic area may be identified when reading the literature. For example, Jacobs (1999) observed that no official data exists on criminal offenses committed by police officers. With this knowledge derived from the literature, scholars interested in researching this topic understand that locating data will be problematic to their study.

The literature review is a critical piece of a research project. Reading the available literature will improve the student's knowledge of the topic and may allow them to speak to topic experts. Perhaps most rewarding, though, is the feeling of inclusion derived from the connection between other scholars' work and your own. As noted by Adams et al. (2007), writing the literature review introduces students to an academic community as someone "who can speak and write with confidence and authority on a specific research problem" (p. 39).

Writing the Essay

Presenting the information contained in a research essay in a clear and ordered fashion is essential to the essay's effectiveness. Students may find creating an outline of the essay's major points helpful in organizing the logical flow of ideas. Follow the outline, but do not be afraid to move information if it fits better elsewhere (Kirszner & Mandell, 2011). Every essay should be structured logically with a distinct introduction, body, and conclusion.

The introduction section is usually one paragraph in length, but it may be several paragraphs for longer assignments. The thesis statement is often the last sentence in this paragraph. It is a clearly written, single sentence intended to inform the reader of the writer's main idea.

Body paragraphs support the thesis statement. The writer's ideas are supported by paraphrases and quotations from sources and the writer's opinion (Kirszner & Mandell, 2011). Each paragraph should begin with a clear topic sentence using language identical or similar to the thesis statement and focus on a single idea. The last sentence of each body paragraph should be a transition sentence. This sentence signals the reader that the topic is about to change.

Finally, the conclusion paragraph summarizes the essay. It should include a sentence that restates the thesis statement as a reminder of the writer's main idea. The conclusion should be at least one paragraph, but it may be longer if needed.

Working and Annotated Bibliographies

A working bibliography is a list of sources you consult (Hacker, 2006). The working bibliography is the beginnings of the references page that appears on the last page of the research essay and can be reviewed to relocate source material during the writing process. Researchers often locate many more sources than they actually use, so not all sources identified in a working bibliography will appear on the references page (Hacker, 2006).

The Internet makes creating a working bibliography a relatively simple process. All that is necessary is to capture the author's name, the title of the source, and the URL or reference site where the source was originally located. For example, a student researching the effect of prison architecture on inmate behavior on GS might locate a journal article titled "Prison Architecture and Inmate Misconduct: A Multilevel Assessment." This information can then be copied and pasted into a working bibliography Word document and saved for later reference.

Clicking the quotation mark at the bottom of the source opens a new window containing the complete source information formatted in several reference styles. The APA format for this article is displayed below.

> Morris, R. G., & Worrall, J. L. (2014). Prison architecture and inmate misconduct: A multilevel assessment. *Crime & Delinquency*, *60*(7), 1083–1109.

The annotated bibliography includes more detail than the working bibliography. An annotated bibliography includes the bibliographic details as well as a brief summary of the source content (Wyrick, 2013). The annotated bibliography serves several important purposes. For the student writer, "it demonstrates that you've read your sources and understand them, and it serves as practice for 'real' research" (Brown, 2014, p. 240). For other researchers, an annotated bibliography is a valuable resource. If an annotated bibliography is available in the researcher's topic area, time and effort can be saved in locating source information.

Prison architecture and inmate misconduct: A multilevel assessment   **[PDF]** researchgate.net

RG Morris, JL Worrall - Crime & Delinquency, 2014 - journals.sagepub.com
Researchers have not yet devoted sufficient attention to the effect of **prison architecture** on inmate misconduct. Using data from the population of male prisoners in Texas, the authors explored the association between two **prison** architectural design types (as determined by …
☆ ⁇ Cited by 72   Related articles   All 8 versions

Source: Google and the Google logo are registered trademarks of Google LLC. Used with permission.

Exercise 8.3

1. Enter this URL into a Web browser to access an annotated bibliography on women offenders prepared by the National Institute of Corrections Information Center: http://static.nicic.gov.s3.amazonaws.com/Library/021385.pdf.

2. Refer to the search parameters mentioned earlier in this chapter. Use a search parameter to locate an annotated bibliography on teen dating violence.

Figure 8.1   Sample Student Essay

Domestic Violence in Police Families
Student Name
College/University Name

Introduction

The vast majority of police officers go about the business of their profession in a proficient and honorable manner. Each year, millions of people who have contact with the police overwhelmingly report that officers acted properly and were respectful (see the Bureau of Justice Statistics series "Contacts between the police and public," 1999–2008). Every profession, however, has rogue actors.

Despite a vibrant body of literature exploring police misconduct, few studies of crimes committed by police officers exist. Most are limited by a dearth of data or focus upon the actions of officers within a single department. Jacobs (1999) lamented that despite significant resources invested in the police and measuring crime, no official data on criminal acts committed by officers exists leaving scholars, policymakers, and the public data deprived. The lack of data leaves scholars struggling to understand police criminality (Chappell & Piquero, 2004; Dunn & Caceres, 2010; Eitle, D'Alessio, & Stolzenberg, 2014), but the media are at no loss for dramatic accounts of officer misconduct. A simple Google News search for "police officer arrested" returns over 700,000 news reports, which may lead readers to conclude that crime committed by officers is pervasive and erode the public trust. Sounding official, the CATO Institute maintains the National Police Misconduct Reporting Project (see http://www.policemisconduct.net/), but it, too, is based on local news reports. Absent credible data, even scholars have turned to the news in search of information on officers involved in criminal acts.

Domestic violence committed by police officers

Few studies of domestic crime committed by police officers exist, but those that do suggest the frequency of domestic violence is at least as high as or higher among police families than the general population (IACP, 2003; Truman & Morgan, 2014). One study claims that 40 percent of police families experience domestic violence (Neidig, Russell, & Seng, 1992, p. 30), a rate more than twice that experienced in the general population (Truman & Morgan, 2014, p. 1). Another study suggests that in departments serving populations of over 100,000, 55 percent of agencies had a policy directed at handling domestic violence calls involving police officers (as cited in Erwin, Gershon, Tiburzi, & Lin, 2005, p. 14) suggesting police administrators recognize a problem exists.

Explaining domestic violence in police families

Several studies attempt to identify officer-level attributes that may contribute to domestic violence. One study identified demographics for those officers involved in domestic violence cases in a large, urban department. The majority of officers were minority male patrol officers with a mean age of 34 years. These officers had worked in policing for about 8 years and were typically assigned to high-crime areas (Erwin, Gershon, Tiburzi, & Lin, 2005, p. 15). Additionally, the authors found that most complaints (48 percent) were filed against the officer by the officer's wife followed by the officer's ex-wife or ex-girlfriend (27 percent) and their present girlfriend (22 percent). Most complaints alleged simple battery (77 percent), and a number of officers had a history of at least one previous complaint of domestic violence (23 percent) (Erwin, Gershon, Tiburzi, & Lin, 2005, p. 17). Of the study group members, most were either immediately suspended (64 percent) or arrested (26 percent). Just eight percent of these cases, though, resulted in any final formal action due to a lack of support from the victim (61 percent) or a lack of evidence (31 percent) (Erwin, Gershon, Tiburzi, & Lin, 2005, p. 17).

The impact of officer malpractice

Several studies suggest the media play a role in shaping public opinion. The great bulk of police work is isolated from the public's view, and much of what the public knows about the police is derived from the media (Dowler, 2003, p. 112). Repeated exposure to numerous media accounts of misconduct may lead viewers to believe the behavior is rampant (Weitzer, & Tuch, 2004, p. 308-309) and is strongly correlated with citizen perception of police conduct (Weitzer, & Tuch, 2004, p. 321). Chermak, McGarrell, and Gruenewald, (2006) found the more a person read news accounts of officer misconduct, the more likely they felt the officer was guilty (p. 272).

Responses to domestic violence by police officers

Perhaps most instrumental in revealing the problem of domestic violence acts committed by police officers was the federal Omnibus Consolidated Appropriations Act of 1996, otherwise known as the Lautenberg Amendment. The Amendment altered the Gun Control Act of 1968, which was designed to prevent the use of guns in domestic violence situations (Halstead, 2001, p. 2). Its most significant effect on police officers is that it removed the "public service" exemption, which previously allowed local, state, and federal officers to continue to carry and use firearms for employment-related duties (Halstead, 2001, p. 2). This retroactive act, though, made it illegal for anyone convicted of a domestic violence crime involving physical violence or a firearm, including police officers, from owning or using a firearm (Johnson, Todd, & Subramanian, 2005, p. 3). This legislation forced agencies that may have previously ignored or informally addressed domestic violence within their ranks to identify past offenders and review and update agency policies on handling cases when the suspect is an officer (Johnson, Todd, & Subramanian, 2005, p. 3).

Conclusion

The purpose of this paper was to survey the available literature in an effort to better understand what is known about domestic violence in police families, its predictors, and the criminal justice system response to events when they occur. While few studies exist that examine domestic violence that occurs in police families, a number of studies suggest the rate of domestic violence committed by police officers may be higher than that of the general population.

While no profession is without its rogue actors, officers who commit acts of domestic violence must be dealt with swiftly in order to protect victims and the public trust. Successful policing is based on a relationship of trust between the police and the community they serve, for "(w)ithout trust between police and citizens, effective policing is impossible" (United States Department of Justice, 1994, pg. vii).

(Continued)

Figure 8.1 (Continued).

References**

Barnett, O. W., Miller-Perrin, C. L., & Perrin, R. D. (2011). *Family violence across the lifespan: An introduction.* Thousand Oaks, CA: Sage

Blackwell, B. S., & Vaughn, M. S. (2003). Police civil liability for inappropriate response to domestic assault victims. *Journal of Criminal Justice, 31*(2), 129–146.

Castle Rock v. Gonzales, 545 U.S. 04–278 (2005).

Çelik, A. (2013). An analysis of mandatory arrest policy on domestic violence. *International Journal Of Human Sciences, 10*(1), 1503-1523.

Chappell, A. T., & Piquero, A. R. (2004). Applying social learning theory to police misconduct. *Deviant Behavior, 25*(2), 89-108.

Chermak, S., McGarrell, E., & Gruenewald, J. (2006). Media coverage of police misconduct and attitudes toward police. *Policing, 29*(2), 261-281.

Dowler, K. (2003). Media consumption and public attitudes toward crime and justice: The relationship between fear of crime, punitive attitudes, and perceived police effectiveness. *Journal of Criminal Justice and Popular Culture,10*(2), 109-126.

Dunn, A., & Caceres, P. J. (2010). Constructing a better estimate of police misconduct. *Policy Matters Journal,* Spring, 10-16.

** Partial Reference list

CHAPTER SUMMARY

This chapter introduced students to writing an academic essay using credible sources. Writing a successful essay begins with understanding the assignment due dates, including those before the final essay is submitted. Creating a writing schedule can help students meet these deadlines. Students should select a topic and focus the research questions to a topic area in which a sufficient body of literature exists to support the thesis. Literature can be found using primary and secondary sources identified through the Internet, library resources, criminal justice databases, and news sources. Students must critically analyze these sources for its respect as a scholarly source, as well as its reliability, currency, and credibility. By following the guidance contained in this chapter, students should find writing an academic essay a rewarding and educational experience.

ADDITIONAL READING

1. "Writing a Research Paper." Available at https://owl.english.purdue.edu/owl/resource/658/01/.

2. "Writing a Research Paper." Available at https://writing.wisc.edu/Handbook/PlanResearchPaper.html.

QUESTIONS FOR CONSIDERATION

1. The research essay is similar to other types of essays. What is a major difference between the research essay and other essays?

2. List and describe the four questions a student should ask when evaluating sources.

3. Define primary source and secondary source. Include a discussion of the advantages and disadvantages of each.

4. Discuss the advantages of using country codes for a search.

5. Visit a criminal justice database. Describe the information that can be found on the site and discuss how this information can benefit your research.

EXERCISE ANSWERS

Exercise 8.2 Answers

1. The American War for Independence

2. The Great Patriotic War

3. First page results for UK sites focus on gun control, while U.S. results focus on gun ownership.

References

Adams, A., Kahn, H., Raeside, R., & White, D. (2007). *Research methods for graduate students and social science students*. Thousand Oaks, CA: Sage.

Albitz, R. S. (2007). The what and who of information literacy and critical thinking in higher education. *portal: Libraries and the Academy, 7*(1), 97–109.

Alleyne, R. (2011, February 11). Welcome to the information age—174 newspapers a day. *The Telegraph*. Retrieved from http://www.telegraph.co.uk/news/science/science-news/8316534/Welcome-to-the-information-age-174-newspapers-a-day.html.

American Library Association. (2018). Digital literacy definition. Retrieved from http://connect.ala.org/node/181197.

American Psychological Association. (2010). *Publication manual of the American Psychological Association* (6th ed.). Washington, DC: Author.

American Psychological Association. (2018). Ethical principles of psychologists and code of conduct. American Psychological Association Ethics Office. Retrieved from http://www.apa.org/ethics/code/.

Angeli, E., Wagner, J., Lawrick, E., Moore, K., Anderson, M., Soderlund, L., & Brizee, A. (2010, May 5). General format. Retrieved from http://owl.english.purdue .edu/owl/resource/560/01/.

Arizona v. Gant, 129 S. Ct. 1710 (2009).

Arizona v. Johnson, 555 U.S. 323 (2009).

Association of College and Research Libraries. (2000). Information literacy competency standards for higher education. Retrieved from http://www.ala.org/Template .cfm?Section=Home&template=/ContentManagement/ContentDisplay.cfm&ContentID=33553.

Astolfi, C. (2016). Case dismissed, inmate released due to bad search warrant. *Sandusky Register*. Retrieved from http://www.sanduskyregister.com/story/ 201610140035.

Bailey, J. (2012). 5 famous plagiarists: Where are they now? *Plagiarism Today*. Retrieved from https://www .plagiarismtoday.com/2012/08/21/5-famous-plagiarists-where-are-they-now/.

Baldick, C. (1996). *Oxford dictionary of literary terms*. Oxford, UK: Oxford University Press.

Baxter, D. (2016). Thousands of fake ballot slips found marked for Hillary Clinton. Retrieved from https://yournewswire.com/thousands-ballot-slips-hillary-clinton/.

Berekmer v. McCarty, 468 U.S. 420 (1984).

Biber, D., & Gray, B. (2010). Challenging stereotypes about academic writing: Complexity, elaboration, explicitness. *Journal of English for Academic Purposes, 9*(1), 2–20.

Bombaro, C. (2012). *Finding history: Research methods and resources for students and scholars*. Lanham, MD: Scarecrow Press.

Breivik, P. (2005). 21st century learning and information literacy. *Change, 37*(2), 20–27.

Brewer, M., & American Library Association Office for Information Technology Policy. (2012). Digital copyright slider. Retrieved from http://librarycopyright. net/resources/digitalslider/index.html.

Brown, L. (2014). *How to write anything: A complete guide*. New York, NY: W.W. Norton.

Business Communication. (2018). The importance of the business letter. Retrieved from https://thebusiness-communication.com/importance-of-business-letter/.

Byrd v. United States, 528 U.S. ____ (2018).

CareerBuilding.com. (2017). Number of employers using social media to screen candidates at all-time high, finds latest CareerBuilding study. Retrieved from https://www .prnewswire.com/news-releases/number-of-employers-using-social-media-to-screen-candidates-at-all-time-high-finds-latest-careerbuilder-study- 300474228.html.

Cathcart, R., & Roberts, A. (2006). Evaluating Google Scholar as a tool for information literacy. Retrieved from https://fau.digital.flvc.org/islandora/object/fau%3A7550/datastream/OBJ/view/Evaluating_Google_Scholar_as_a_tool_for_information_literacy.pdf.

Center for Disease Control and Prevention. (n.d.). DES research: Deciding whether a source is reliable. Retrieved from https://www.cdc.gov/des/consumers/research/understanding_deciding.html.

City of Indianapolis v. Edmond, 531 U.S. 32 (2000).

CNN.com. (2003). *New York Times*: Reporter routinely faked articles. *CNN.com*. Retrieved from http://www .cnn.com/2003/US/Northeast/05/10/ny.times.reporter/

Collins v. Virginia, 524 U.S. ____ (2018).

Crossick, G. (2016). Monographs and open access. *Insights, 29*(1), 14–19.

Davis, M. S. (1999). *Grantsmanship for criminal justice and criminology*. Thousand Oaks, CA: Sage.

Davis v. United States, 328 U.S. 582 (1946).

Department of Justice. (2018). Grants. Retrieved from https://www.justice.gov/grants.

Dissell, R. (2010). Words used in sexual assault police reports can help or hurt cases. *The Plains Dealer*. Retrieved from http://blog.cleveland.com/metro/2010/07/words_used_in_sexual_assault_p.html.

Doyle, A. (2018a). How to format a business letter. Retrieved from https://www.thebalancecareers.com/how-to-format-a-business-letter-2062540.

Doyle, A. (2018b). Tips for formatting a cover letter for a resume. *The Balance Careers*. Retrieved from https://www.thebalancecareers.com/how-to-format-a-cover-letter-2060170.

Eastern Illinois University. (2016). Scholarly monographs. Retrieved from https://booth.library.eiu.edu/subjectsPlus/subjects/guide.php?subject=monographs.

EBSCO. (2018). Newspaper source. Retrieved from https://www.ebsco.com/products/research-databases/newspaper-source.

Ennis, R. (2011). *The nature of critical thinking: An outline of critical thinking dispositions and abilities*. Retrieved from http://faculty.education.illinois.edu/rhennis/documents/TheNatureofCriticalThinking_51711_000.pdf.

Federal Bureau of Investigation. (n.d.a). About the UCR program. Retrieved from https://www.fbi.gov/file-repository/ucr/about-the-ucr-program.pdf/view.

Federal Bureau of Investigation. (n.d.b). Guidelines for preparation of fingerprint cards and associated criminal history information. Retrieved from https://www.fbi.gov/file-repository/guidelines-for-preparation-of-fingerprint-cards-and-association-criminal-history-information.pdf/view.

Federal Bureau of Investigation. (n.d.c). *National Incident-Based Reporting System user manual*. UCR Publications. Retrieved from https://www.fbi.gov/services/cjis/ucr/publications#Crime-in%20the%20U.S.

Federal Register. (2018). Federal policy for the protection of human subjects: Delay of the revisions to the federal policy for the protection of human subjects. *Federal Register, The Daily Journal of the United States Government*. Interim Final Rule. Retrieved from https://www.federalregister.gov/documents/2018/01/22/2018-00997/federal-policy-for-the-protection-of-human-subjects-delay-of-the-revisions-to-the-federal-policy-for#_blank.

Flaherty, M. P., & Harriston, K. A. (1994). Police credibility on trial in D. C. courts. *Washington Post*. Retrieved from http://www.washingtonpost.com/wp-srv/local/longterm/library/dc/dcpolice/94series/trainingday3.htm?noredirect=on.

Florida Department of Highway Safety and Motor Vehicles. (2017). *Traffic crash facts: Annual report 2016*. Available at https://flhsmv.gov/pdf/crashreports/crash_facts_2016.pdf.

Gale, P. (2014). Effective business writing: Top principles and techniques. English Grammar. Retrieved from https://www.englishgrammar.org/effective-business-writing/.

Gallo, A. (2014). How to write a cover letter. Retrieved from https://hbr.org/2014/02/how-to-write-a-cover-letter.

Garcia, A., & Lear, J. (2016, November 2). 5 stunning fake news stories that reached millions. *CNN Money*. Retrieved from http://money.cnn.com/2016/11/02/media/fake-news-stories/index.html.

Garner, B. A. (2013). *HBR guide to better business writing*. Boston, MA: Harvard Business Review Press.

Georgetown University Library. (2018). Evaluating Internet resources. Retrieved from https://www.library.georgetown.edu/tutorials/research-guides/evaluating-internet-content.

Google Scholar (n.d.). About Google Scholar. Retrieved from https://scholar.google.com/intl/en/scholar/about.html.

Hacker, D. (2006). *The Bedford handbook* (7th ed.). Boston, MA: Bedford/St. Martin.

Hancock, D. R., & Algozzine, B. (2016). *Doing case study research: A practical guide for beginning researchers*. New York, NY: Teachers College Press.

Haner, J., Wilson, K., & O'Donnell, J. (2002). Cases crumble, killers go free. *The Baltimore Sun*. Retrieved from http://www.baltimoresun.com/bal-te.murder-29sep 29-story.html.

Harrison, J., Weisman, D., & Zornado, J. L. (2017). *Professional writing for the criminal justice system*. New York, NY: Springer Publishing Company. Retrieved from http://proxygsu-abr1.galileo.usg.edu/login?url=http://search.ebscohost.com/login.aspx?direct=true&db=nlebk&AN=1507663&site=eds-live&scope=site.

Harvard Extension School. (2017–2018). Tips to avoid plagiarism. Harvard University. Retrieved from https://www.extension.harvard.edu/resources-policies/resources/tips-avoid-plagiarism.

Harvey, W. L. (2015). Leadership quotes and police truisms. Retrieved from https://www.officer.com/training-careers/article/12057342/leadership-quotes-and-police-truisms#platformComments.

Heitin, L. (2016). What is digital literacy? *Education Week, 36*(12), 5–6.

Hilbert, M., & Lopez, P. (2011). The world's technological capacity to store, communicate, and compute information. *Science, 332*(6025), 60–65. Retrieved from http://science.sciencemag.org/content/332/6025/60.

Hunt, E. (2016, December 17). What is fake news? How to spot it and what you can do to stop it. *The Guardian.* Retrieved from https://www.theguardian.com/media/2016/dec/18/what-is-fake-news-pizzagate.

Illinois v. Cabales, 543 U.S. 405 (2005).

Illinois v. Lidster, 540 U.S. 419 (2004).

Jacobs, J. B. (1999). Dilemmas of corruption control. *Perspectives on Crime & Justice, 3,* 73–93.

Karsh, E., & Fox, A. S. (2014). *The only grant-writing book you'll ever need.* New York, NY: Basic Books.

Kellogg, R. T. (2008). Training writing skills: A cognitive developmental perspective. *Journal of Writing Research, 1*(1), 1–26.

Kirszner, L. G., & Mandell, S. R. (2011). *Patterns for college writing: A rhetorical reader and guide.* Boston, MA: Bedford/St. Martin's.

Kleckner, M. J., & Marshall, C. R. (2014). Critical communication skills: Developing course competencies to meet workforce needs. *The Journal of Research in Business Education, 56*(2), 59.

Kong, S. C. (2014). Developing information literacy and critical thinking skills through domain knowledge learning in digital classrooms: An experience of practicing flipped classroom strategy. *Computers & Education, 78,* 160–173.

Larson, A. (2016). What is Megan's law. Retrieved from https://www.expertlaw.com/library/criminal/megans_law.html.

Legal Information Institute. (n.d.a). Arrest warrant or summons on a complaint. Retrieved from https://www.law.cornell.edu/rules/frcrmp/rule_4.

Legal Information Institute. (n.d.b). Search warrant. Retrieved from https://www.law.cornell.edu/wex/search_warrant.

Lentz, P. (2013). MBA students' workplace writing: Implications for business writing pedagogy and workplace practice. *Business Communication Quarterly, 76*(4), 474–490.

Leo, R. A. (2009). *Police interrogation and American justice.* Cambridge, MA: Harvard University Press.

LexisNexis. (n.d.). LexisNexis academic. Retrieved from https://www.lexisnexis.com/en-us/products/lexisnexis-academic.page.

Lohr, D. (2017). Crimes that dominated headlines in 2017. Huffington Post. Retrieved from https://www.huffingtonpost.com/entry/crimes-that-dominated-headlines-in-2017_us_5a3acc5ee4b0b0e5a79f4b53.

Maryland v. Macon, 472 U.S. 463 (1985).

McAllister, C., & Louth, R. (1988). The effect of word processing on the quality of basic writers' revisions. *Research in the teaching of English, 22*(4), 417.

McLoughlin, C. (1995).Tertiary literacy: A constructivist perspective. Open Letter. *Australian Journal for Adult Literacy, Research and Practice, 5*(2), 27–42.

Melé, D. (2009). *Business ethics in action: Seeking human excellence in organizations.* London, United Kingdom: Palgrave Macmillan.

Merriam-Webster's Dictionary. (2018). Ethics. Retrieved from https://www.merriam-webster.com/dictionary/ethic.

Michigan Dept. of State Police v. Sitz, 496 U.S. 444 (1990).

Minnesota v. Carter, 525 U.S. 83 (1998).

Minnesota v. Dickerson, 508 U.S. 366 (1993).

Modern Language Association. (2018). Works cited: A quick guide. MLA Style Center, Modern Language Association. Retrieved from https://style.mla.org/works-cited-a-quick-guide/.

Murgado, A. (2016). How to obtain a sworn statement. *Police: The Law Enforcement Magazine.* Retrieved from http://www.policemag.com/channel/patrol/articles/2016/08/how-to-obtain-a-sworn-statement.aspx.

National Forum on Information Literacy. (2018). *National forum on information literacy 1999–2000 report.* American Library Association. Retrieved from http://www.ala.org/aboutala/national-forum-information-literacy-1999%E2%80%932000-report.

National Highway Traffic Safety Administration. (n.d.). Fatality reporting system. Retrieved from https://www-fars.nhtsa.dot.gov/Main/index.aspx.

National Highway Traffic Safety Administration. (2017). *Model minimum uniform crash criteria* (5th ed.) Retrieved from https://www.nhtsa.gov/mmucc-1.

National Institute of Corrections. (2018). History. Retrieved from https://nicic.gov/history-of-nic.

National Institute of Justice. (2013). Mapping and analysis for public safety. Retrieved from http://nij.gov/topics/technology/maps/pages/welcome.aspx.

National Institutes of Health. (2017). Rigor and reproducibility. U.S. Department of Health and Human Services. National Institutes of Health. Washington, DC. Retrieved from https://grants.nih.gov/reproducibility/index.htm.

New Jersey v. TLO, 469 U.S. 325 (1985).

Nordquist, R. (2018). What is business writing? Definitions, tips, and examples. ThoughtCo. Retrieved from https://www.thoughtco.com/what-is-business-writing-1689188.

November, A. (2016). The advanced Google searches every student should know. Retrieved form https://novemberlearning.com/educational-resources-for-educators/teaching-and-learning-articles/the-advanced-google-searches-every-student-should-know/.

Ober, S. (1995). *Contemporary business communication*. Boston, MA: Houghton Mifflin.

Office of Justice Programs. (2018). Edward Byrne Memorial Justice Assistance Grant Program. Retrieved from https://www.bja.gov/Jag/index.html.

Paul, R. (1995). *Critical thinking: How to prepare students for a rapidly changing world*. J. Willsen & A. Binker (Eds.). Rohnert Park, CA: Sonoma State University.

Paulas, R. (2016). On the front lines of computer literacy. *Pacific Standard*. The Social Justice Foundation. Retrieved from https://psmag.com/education/this-part-is-called-a-url.

Payton v. New York, 445 U.S. 573 (1980).

Phillips Jr., W. E., & Burrell, D. N. (2009). Decision-making skills that encompass a critical thinking orientation for law enforcement professionals. *International Journal of Police Science & Management, 11*(2), 141–149.

ProCon.org. (2019). Overview: About us. Available at https://www.procon.org/about-us.php.

Purdue University. (n.d.). Copyright infringement penalties. University Copyright Office. Purdue University. Retrieved from https://www.lib.purdue.edu/uco/ CopyrightBasics/penalties.html.

Purdue OWL. (2018a). Annotated bibliographies. Retrieved from https://owl.english.purdue.edu/owl/ owlprint/590/.

Purdue OWL (2018b). Literature review. Retrieved from https://owl.purdue.edu/owl/research_and_citation/apa_style/apa_formatting_and_style_guide/types_of_apa_papers.html.

Purdue OWL. (2018c). Parts of a memo. Purdue Online Writing Lab. Retrieved from: https://owl.purdue.edu/owl/subject_specific_writing/professional_technical_writing/memos/parts_of_a_memo.html.

Purdue OWL. (2018d). Resume workshop. Retrieved from https://owl.english.purdue.edu/owl/resource/719/1/.

Purdue OWL (2018e). Writing a research paper. Retrieved from https://owl.purdue.edu/owl/general_writing/common_writing_assignments/research_papers/writing_a_ research_paper.html.

Quible, Z. K., & Griffin, F. (2007). Are writing deficiencies creating a lost generation of business writers? *Journal of Education for Business, 83*(1), 32–36.

Ratcliff, C. (2018). What are the most popular search engines? Retrieved from https://searchenginewatch.com /2016/08/08/what-are-the-top-10-most-popular-search-engines/.

Reeves, B. (2010). Local police departments, 2007. U.S. Department of Justice, Office of Justice Programs. Retrieved from https://www.bjs.gov/content/pub/pdf/lpd07.pdf.

Reeves, B. A. (2011). Local police departments. Retrieved from https://bjs.gov/content/pub/pdf/lpd07.pdf.

Reid, S. T. (1997). *Crime and criminology* (8th ed.). Chicago: Brown and Benchmark.

Resnick, D. B. (2015). What is ethics in research and why is it important? National Institute of Environmental Health Sciences. Retrieved from https://www.niehs .nih.gov/research/resources/bioethics/whatis/index.cfm.

Rowe, S. E. (2009). Legal research, legal writing, and legal analysis: Putting law school into practice. *Stetson Law Review, 29,* 1193.

Rugerrio, V. (2003). *Beyond feelings: A guide to critical thinking* (8th ed.). New York, NY: McGraw-Hill.

Rutledge, D. (2016). Serving the search warrant. *Police: The Law Enforcement Magazine*. Retrieved from: http://www.policemag.com/channel/patrol/articles/2016/03/serving-the-search-warrant.aspx.

Schiffhorst, G. J., & Schell, J. F. (1991). *The short handbook for writers*. New York, NY: McGraw-Hill.

Shultz, M. (2007). Comparing test searches in PubMed and Google Scholar. *Journal of the Medical Library Association: JMLA, 95*(4), 442.

Smith, D. (2003). Five principles for research ethics. *Monitor on Psychology, 34*(1), 56. Retrieved from http://www.apa.org/monitor/jan03/principles.aspx.

Stanford's Key to Information Literacy. (2018). What is information literacy? Retrieved from http://skil.stanford.edu/intro/research.html.

Swanson, C. R., Chamelin, N. C., Territo, L., & Taylor, R. W. (2003). *Criminal investigation*. Boston: McGraw-Hill.

Technopedia.com. (2018). Computer literate. Retrieved from https://www.techopedia.com/definition/23303/computer-literate.

Terry v. Ohio, 392 U.S. 1 (1968).

United States Courts. (n.d.). What does the Fourth Amendment mean? Retrieved from http://www.uscourts.gov/about-federal-courts/educational-resources/about-educational-outreach/activity-resources/what-does-0.

United States v. Arvizu, 534 U.S. 266 (2002).

United States v. Montoya de Hernandez, 473 U.S. 531 (1985).

United States v. Robinson, 414 U.S. 218 (1973).

University of Washington–Tacoma. (2018). Criminal justice: Source types: Peer-reviewed & scholarly & more. Retrieved from http://guides.lib.uw.edu/c.php?g=344206&p=2319662.

U.S. Copyright Office. (n.d.). Copyright in general. Retrieved from https://www.copyright.gov/help/faq/faq-general.html#what.

U.S. Department of Justice. (n.d.). UCR offense definitions. Retrieved from https://www.ucrdatatool.gov/offenses.cfm.

U.S. Department of Justice (2014). Georgia police officials and former deputy indicted by federal grand jury on charges of excessive force and obstruction of justice. Retrieved from https://www.justice.gov/opa/pr/georgia-police-officials-and-former-deputy-indicted-federal-grand-jury-charges-excessive

U.S. Department of Justice (2018). *National Incident-Based Reporting System User Manual*. Retrieved from https://www.fbi.gov/file-repository/ucr/ucr-2019-1-nibrs-user-manual.pdf/view.

VandenBos, G. R. (2010). Foreword. In *Publication manual of the American Psychological Association* (6th ed.). Washington, DC: American Psychological Association.

Wadman, R. C., & Allison, W. (2003). *To protect and serve: A history of police in America*. Upper Saddle River, NJ: Prentice Hall.

Ward, D. (2006). Revisioning information literacy for lifelong meaning. *The Journal of Academic Librarianship, 32*, 396–402.

warrant. (n.d.). *Legal dictionary*. Retrieved from https://legaldictionary.net/warrant/.

Weiler, A. (2005). Information-seeking behavior in generation Y students: Motivation, critical thinking, and learning theory. *The Journal of Academic Librarianship, 31*, 46–53.

Weisburd, D., & Lum, C. (2005). The diffusion of computerized crime mapping in policing: Linking research and practice. *Police Practice and Research, 6*(5), 419–434.

Wertz, R. E. H., Fosmire, M., Purzer, S., Saragih, A. I., Van Epps, A. S., Sapp Nelson, M. R., & Dillman, B. G. (2013). *Work in progress: Critical thinking and information literacy: Assessing student performance*. Unpublished manuscript presented at the 12th annual American Society for Engineering Education Conference. Presented at the 120th ASEE Annual Conference & Exposition, Atlanta, GA, American Society for Engineering Education.

Wheeler, L. (2018). Supreme court sets new limits on police searches. *The Hill*. Retrieved from https://thehill.com/regulation/court-battles/389697-supreme-court-sets-new-limits-on-police-searches.

Wikipedia: About. (2018). Wikipedia.org. https://en.wikipedia.org/wiki/Wikipedia: About.

Wonacott, M. E. (2001). Technological literacy. ERIC Digest. Retrieved from https://www.ericdigests.org/2002-3/literacy.htm. Eric Identifier ED459371.

Writing Center of Wisconsin-Madison. (2018). Writing cover letters. Retrieved from https://writing.wisc.edu/Handbook/CoverLetters.html.

Wyrick, J. (2013). *Steps to writing well with additional readings*. Boston, MA: Wadsworth.